TUSCANY
FROM THE AIR

The photographer wishes to dedicate this book to his mother, Cornelia.

Pages 4-5: The Tuscan hills are distinguished by a unique gentleness,
which moved a fascinated Henry James to speak of their "magic atmosphere".

Pages 6-7: A white road, bordered by tall, severe cypresses,
snakes through the countryside: a typical Tuscan scene,
unchanged over the centuries.

Pages 8-9: With its colours and lines, Tuscany often seems to practise
the art of painting, using every means of expression
to communicate its unique message.

Pages 10-11: San Gimignano and its famous towers.
The town's glorious past remains alive, almost untouched by time.

Translated from the Italian by John Tuttle

Edited by Barbara Rosen

Designed by Louise Brody

First published in United States in 1991 by
Thames & Hudson Inc, 500 Fifth Avenue
New York, New York 10110

Copyright © 1990 Editions Didier Millet

Library of Congress Catalog Card Number 91 - 65318

Printed and bound by Tien Wah Press Singapore
Colour separation : Colourscan Singapore

TUSCANY
FROM THE AIR

GIUSEPPE GRAZZINI
PHOTOGRAPHS BY GUIDO ALBERTO ROSSI

THAMES AND HUDSON

CONTENTS

F*lorence in an eighteenth-century painting. This was a happy period for Tuscany: the last of the Medici, Giangastone, died in 1747, ending the dynasty of that great family, and Tuscany passed to the Grand Dukes of Lorraine. Thus began an era of economic initiatives and sweeping administrative reforms, including the undertaking of great public works like the draining of the swamps.*

A
TUSCAN AIR

T o honour Tuscany, with its glorious history, perhaps one should use its ancient name, Etruria. Thus one thinks immediately of the kingdom the Etruscans built, rather than of the region the Romans conquered. Despite their power, their glory and their prosperity, the inhabitants of the Etruscan kingdom have always remained an enigmatic people: practically nothing is known of their origins, apart from the fact that they belonged to none of the ancient Italic races of the peninsula. According to Herodotus, the Etruscans came to central Italy from Lydia, an ancient region on the Turkish coast of the Aegean Sea. However, they were not of direct Lydian descent; it is thought their ancestors may have been the Pelasgian navigators who, according to legend, populated Greece and nearby lands in ancient times. Some historians maintain that the Etruscans arrived overland from Asia via Central Europe, while others even claim they came from mythical Atlantis.

One thing we do know is that the Etruscan language bore no relation to the Indo-European tongues that formed the basis of those spoken by the native Italic peoples. The only similar language is a dialect, itself atypical, that was still spoken in the sixth century BC on the Greek island of Lemnos.

Between the seventh and sixth centuries BC, the Etruscans' power extended over a large part of Italy from the Po Valley to Campania. This empire included such cities as Felsina (later Bologna); Spina, in the Po delta on the Adriatic; and Capua, further south and on the edge of Latium. Etruscan vessels sailed from such ports as Caere (today Cerveteri), Vulci and Populonia, vying for Mediterranean supremacy with the Phoenicians, Greeks and Carthaginians. And it was around the Etruscan banner that the Italic peoples rallied in their desperate, final resistance to the Romans, whose conquest, in fact, was not fully achieved until the first century BC.

Although the language of the invaders transformed them into "Tusci" and finally "Toscani", the former Etruscans have retained a strong sense of their history, as well as their ancestors' physical

characteristics: a narrow nose, long nostrils and thin lips arched in a vaguely disdainful expression. This is why Tuscany has never, in any sense, been a transitional region between north and south Italy but has remained proudly individualist and self-sufficient. The least attractive attribute of this attitude, it must be admitted, is a certain arrogance towards the inhabitants of the rest of the peninsula.

The modern-day Italian language originated in Tuscany where the vulgate, evolving from the decadent structures of late Latin, attained its highest literary expression. The Sicilian school of poetry, which flourished at the cultivated court of the Emperor Frederick II in Palermo, was developing similar linguistic reforms during the thirteenth century. But it was the Tuscan Italian of *The Divine Comedy*, masterpiece of the Florentine Dante Alighieri, that grew into a national language. Today Tuscan literary primacy remains unquestioned, even by writers from other regions.

Along with a jealously defended identity, Tuscan individualism persisted undaunted from the fall of the Roman Empire through the barbarian invasions and the rise of the free Communes of the Middle Ages. It was also a source of internal political fragmentation. The individualist tendency was taken up by every city and, within every city, in every neighbourhood, by every family and by every member of every family. Medieval factions multiplied and spun off into opposing tendencies, as in the case of Florence's Guelphs who, after warring against the Ghibellines, disputed amongst themselves and finally split into the White and Black Guelphs. Tuscany's history is a many-tiered succession of conspiracies, treasons and long internecine battles followed by brokered truces. It was only with the rise of the great ruling seigniories – the outstanding example, of course, being the Medici in Florence – that the region began to enjoy periods of peace. These were always too brief, but they were nonetheless long enough to allow the flowering of arts, letters and sciences.

Even centuries later, national unity (on paper if not in spirit) would fail to bring Tuscany any further into the Italian fold. In the nineteenth century Florence was chosen capital of Victor Emmanuel II's Kingdom of Italy. But this short-lived (1865-71) honour did nothing to make Tuscany any less "foreign" vis-à-vis the rest of the country. All of Europe, including Florence, knew the House of Savoy had chosen Florence merely to show the world that it was getting close to Rome, the natural capital geographically and historically. So Florence received the king with the same indifference it showed other outside sovereigns, although mixed with some regret for the previous, more enlightened government of the Grand Dukes of Lorraine.

Since this time Tuscany has changed in many ways, but its people remain as independent, irascible, mocking and argumentative – though also brilliant and, in their own way, charming – as ever. Old rivalries live on, sublimated in the rituals which, despite what tourists might think, represent more than just a touch of "local colour". In the famous Palio horse-race, jockeys from Siena's different districts whip their adversaries more violently than their steeds, and victory is pointless if the vanquished have not been subjected to proper scorn and humiliation. This is only one example of a persistent, atavistic taste for brawling.

Pisa's Mezzogiorno and Tramontana districts still compete in the annual Gioco del Ponte, which dates from the fifteenth century. Each team tries to push a wagon – and the other team

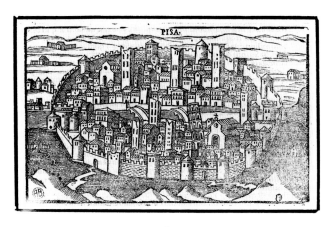

Pisa, in an old engraving. According to scholars, the city was founded by Greek traders between the seventh and sixth centuries BC. Dissenting opinions hold that the founders were Ligurians or Etruscans. A naval base of considerable importance during the Roman era, Pisa had its age of glory between 1000 and 1284, when its fleet dominated a large part of the Mediterranean. Its decline began in 1284, when rival Genoa won the naval Battle of Meloria.

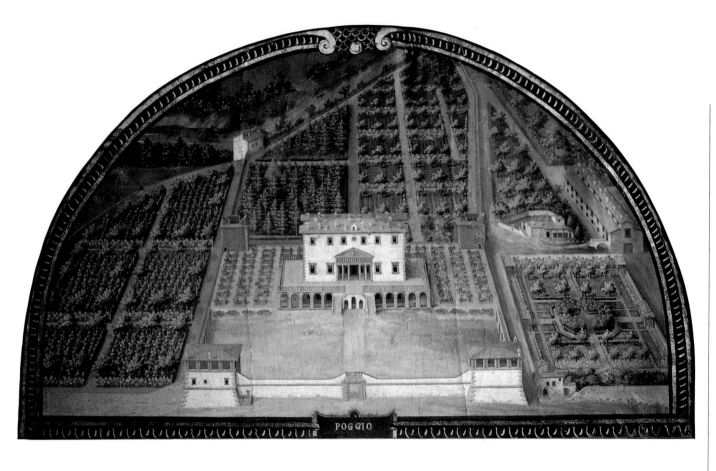

POGGIO

Two typical Medici villas – Poggio and Lambrogiana (below) – depicted in two famous lunettes painted by Giusto Utens in the former convent of the Oblates in Florence. The convent now houses the Firenze Come Era, or Florence As She Was, Museum. The painter, of Flemish roots, was born in Carrara and remained active until his death in 1609. His son Domenico also was a painter and continued his father's work; some of the younger Utens' valuable works are conserved in the Madonna delle Lacrime (Our Lady of Tears) church in Carrara.

LAMBROGIANA

Two more Medici villas – Marignolle and La Peggio (below) – painted by Utens in the Oblates convent in Florence. The pictural cycle of Medici villas dates from 1598-99, during the reign of Grand Duke Cosimo II, and constitutes a precious documentation of the period's history and economics, as well as its art. The villas were splendid residences built to delight the master, who also had to administer the farms that provided his wealth.

MARIGNOLLE

LA PEGGIO

– across a bridge. If an adversary happens to take an unexpected bath, so much the better. This bridge game originated when Lorenzo the Magnificent sought a means of maintaining public peace, since men from the two districts regularly fought with clubs on the Piazza dei Cavalieri, leaving dead and wounded. (It should be noted that this rivalry derives solely from the fact that one district lies on the left bank of the Arno, the other on the right.)

In Tuscany, however, a river is not a prerequisite for a rivalry. The inhabitants of the hillside town of Fucecchio vie across the twenty-five metres that separate the upper part of the town from the lower. Those of the upper part (*in sù*) are known as the *Insuesi*, those of the lower (*in giù*) the *Ingiuesi*. Local disputes were documented as early as the eleventh century. Indro Montanelli, the journalist and native of Fucecchio, relates how even after the Second World War the marriage of members of rival factions would create disturbances worthy of Romeo and Juliet's Verona.

The good people of Leghorn have taken this confrontational tendency to a level all their own. Subjected to Pisan domination in the thirteenth century, their rancour towards their former oppressors remains undiminished today and has evolved into a ferocious, though nonchalant, sarcasm. Leghorn is surely the only town in the world that prints a periodical whose sole editorial policy is to ridicule a neighbouring city. *Il Vernacoliere* often tends to be downright obscene, but given its vigorous good humour it is difficult not to be amused. A rare non-obscene article appeared after the Chernobyl disaster, purportedly dealing with the horrifying effects of radiation poisoning. The banner headline announced: "An intelligent Pisan born!" The subtitle continued: "The world astounded, Tuscany frightened."

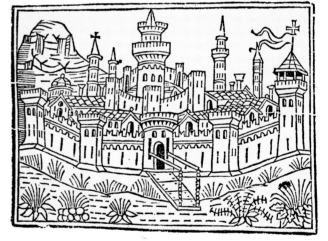

Pistoia, *in another old engraving. The Romans founded this military outpost along the Via Cassia in the second century* BC, *naming it Pistoria. The city entered history in 62* BC, *when Catilina, a Roman patrician who had attempted to seize power and was denounced by Cicero, came there seeking refuge. Pursued by loyalist troops, he died near the city while fighting alongside his remaining followers.*

If this is one facet of the Tuscan character, it is only fair to note others: Tuscans can be nobly generous, even if they are poor. They also are hard-working, tenacious and resourceful. These qualities have contributed to the extraordinary economic development of a region that has steadfastly refused to limit itself to a rural destiny.

The components of Tuscany's growth are varied and, perhaps surprisingly, big industry has not played a significant role. It exists, of course, but it is not really considered Tuscan. The initiatives and capital have tended to come from outside the region. The real fortunes of the Tuscan economy come from its highly specialized, small- and medium-sized businesses, which are often family-run. Thanks to such enterprises, as well as to the service industries (especially trade, Tuscany's glory since the Middle Ages), the region's economy is healthy. It could absolutely thrive if the greatest local resource, tourism, were freed from an inefficient and indecisive bureaucracy.

Upon closer study, one can see how the Tuscan landscape has mirrored political and

The upper painting, by an unknown artist, depicts the solemn entry of Cosimo I de' Medici into Siena in 1561. Siena's glorious Republic had just surrendered to rival Florence which, with the treaty of Cateau-Cambrésis, acquired the entire state, except for the ports of Orbetello, Talamone, Port'Ercole, Argentario and Santo Stefano, which became part of the domain of Naples.
Below: A plan of the city of Lucca, from a sixteenth-century engraving.

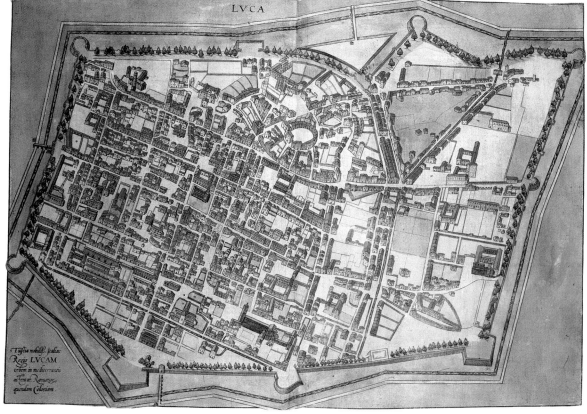

economic evolution, changing gradually but profoundly. Prehistoric Tuscany, covered by forests and marshes, is gone. The pine forest in Versilia is all that remains of the conifer woods which, blended with Mediterranean scrub, once extended all the way to the coast.

The landscape first felt the mark of man with the founding of the Etruscan cities of Fiesole, Volterra, Arezzo, Siena, Cortona, Populonia, Vetulonia, Roselle, Volsinii, Vulci, Pyrgi and Tarquinia. Centuries later, the Romans enlarged existing cities and built new ones such as Florence, clearing swamps, redirecting water flows and cutting back forests. Orderly cultivation imposed new colours and shapes on the countryside. Villas appeared, the grand residences of the conquerors, surrounded by the dwellings of serfs who administered or cultivated the property.

The Roman villa, as described by Cato, Columella and other Latin authors, had a precise, functional structure: around a central courtyard were the baths and kitchen on the south side, the *torcularium* (olive press) and granary on the east, the wine cellar on the north, and the living space on the west. Stalls and stables were outside. Medieval architecture evolved from this form. As the Roman Empire declined, and with it stability, individuals and communities found themselves in constant danger. Castles were built, based upon the same defensive, enclosed plan of the villa. The nobleman's castle, typically on a hill, was flanked by the church and surrounded by the crude dwellings of the common people. Solid walls rendered it unassailable once the drawbridge was raised and the heavy gates closed. Farmland was brought close to these walls so that man and beast could seek refuge quickly in the event of enemy attack.

Thus the undulating harmony of the Tuscan hills was disturbed by the vertical lines of towers and crenellations. Reminders of this dramatic isolation are still prominent today, especially from the air. What appears up close to be a labyrinth of tiny streets emerges, from on high, as an ingenious network of reciprocal protection: the medieval community huddled around the local lord for its own safety as well as his. This relationship influenced every aspect of regional life. The economy was radically transformed. As towns and villages turned in upon themselves commerce, which once ranged freely around the Roman Empire, was reduced to exchange within the immediate area. On those occasions when a Tuscan was forced to venture forth, he risked not only his merchandise and purse but also his life on routes infested with highwaymen, wolves and bears. These dangers pushed towns to adopt economies as self-sufficient as possible, thus returning much of the landscape to its primal beauty.

By the end of the Middle Ages, the scene was changing again with the spread of a system whereby the tenant farmer worked for the landowner as well as for himself, with the aim of

T̲his fifteenth-century engraving shows Pontremoli, a rich stop-over on the Via Francigena between northern Europe and Rome. Already flourishing during the Middle Ages, it is now an important hub of Lunigiana, on the northern border between Tuscany and Liguria. For more than five centuries, Pontremoli has been known as the capital of itinerant booksellers: every year one of Italy's most prestigious literary prizes is awarded there – appropriately called the Bancarella, or Stall.

19

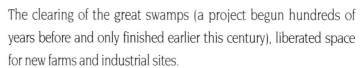

A *medieval engraving showing Cortona, one of the most famous art centres of Tuscany. Cortona has conserved a medieval aspect almost intact, but its origins are in fact Etruscan, as shown by the remains of the first city walls, made of enormous blocks of stone. Even today, it is difficult to understand how the Etruscans, relying on the strength of just their arms and their animals, managed to position such heavy stones.*

eventually earning his own piece of land. Farming again spread into the valleys, where it flourished amid the increasing stability provided by feudal lords and monastic orders and later, by the Florentine seigniory. Scattered dwellings began to dot the Tuscan landscape. The land was now producing more and increasingly varied crops, the scenery becoming richer, as the tenant farmer, preoccupied with raising yields, experimented with all manner of cultivation.

During the Renaissance period, progress in firearms rendered the old, angular castles vulnerable and the architecture was modified, curves being more resistant to bombardment. Then, as diplomats became more useful, and less expensive, than armies, defensive architecture took on the elegance and comfort of the private residence. The castle evolved into the palace: large windows appeared, even in the outer walls, and lovely gardens were laid out within. Such palaces were built inside the cities while, in the country, villas based on the Roman model began to appear.

Commerce became free-ranging again. Along the principal trade routes the Knights Templar opened inns that doubled as trading centres. At these *magioni* one could find food and lodging, hire horses or procure arms simply by presenting a letter. A decisive impetus to trade came in the second half of the sixteenth century with the opening of the Medici Grand Duke's port at Leghorn.

The clearing of the great swamps (a project begun hundreds of years before and only finished earlier this century), liberated space for new farms and industrial sites.

Little by little the old tenant agricultural system disappeared, to be replaced by individual enterprises: small- and medium-sized family-owned farms, or industrial, often foreign-held large-scale holdings. This latter kind of agriculture has changed the Tuscan countryside the most radically. The demands of the marketplace have brought about the disappearance of the mixture of major and minor crops. Gone are the days of green grapevines interspersed by the pale blue flowers of potato-plants, and red tomatoes against silver-grey olives. Now what matters is that machines operate as efficiently as possible and that production continue to expand. Rigorous specialization limits vineyards to vines, olive groves to olive trees and so on, be it grain, salad greens or fruit. Although still rich, the palette of colours is no longer blended. The Tuscan landscape has become rational, losing the joyous vitality that was so suggestive of the Impressionists and their Italian cousins, the Macchiaioli.

Yet even today, the bird's-eye view affords some magnificent contrasts: geometric dark-blue fields of cabbages against golden-yellow expanses of grain, punctuated by the explosive red of poppies. The white trace of a dusty road threads its way up a hillside, and the dark cypress trees draw a line between earth and sky.

The dolce vita in Chianti, as imagined by an eighteenth-century artist. Appropriately for the kingdom of wine, this scene shows the grape harvest, with cupids working, playing, drinking and otherwise amusing themselves. In addition to a little Bacchus astride a goat, one can see some of the region's most famous villas: the Brolio castle, Casole in the Elsa Valley, and Lamole, Greve and Panzano.

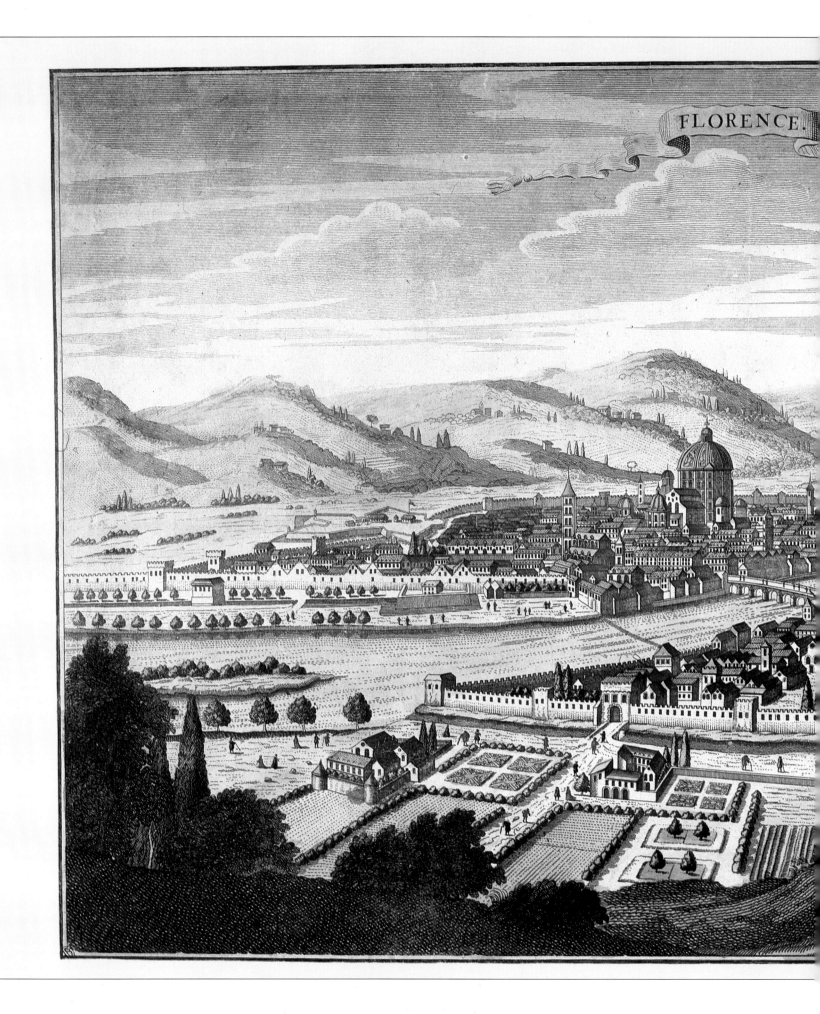

FLORENCE.

22

Florence in an eighteenth-century engraving. Capital of the Grand Duchy of Tuscany by 1569, it was ruled by the Medici until 1738 and then by the House of Lorraine. The city is shown still enclosed within its ancient walls. Immediately beyond is the countryside, rich in cultivated land. The political situation was becoming stable again, and farmhouses were being transformed into sumptuous villas, with large portions of land devoted to elegant gardens.

Santa Maria del Fiore, with Giotto's campanile and the San Giovanni Baptistery. Of these three Florentine monuments, the oldest is the fifth-century Baptistery, whose marble apparently came largely from the remains of a lavish palace dating from the first century. The splendid Duomo, or cathedral, was built between 1296 and 1436. The campanile, begun by Giotto in 1334, was completed by Andrea Pisano and Francesco Talenti in 1359.

THREE

CAPITALS

Florence, Siena and Pisa are the jewels of Tuscany, the three cities that have assured its international reputation. Even if some of their subjects, such as Lucca or Arrezzo, have attempted to compete in the past, they have always bested their rivals and have remained through the centuries the undisputed sovereigns of their glittering domain.

The precise origin of the name Florence (*Firenze* in Italian) remains uncertain. Benvenuto Cellini, the sixteenth-century sculptor, claimed it was named after Fiorinus, one of Julius Caesar's generals. Martial origins would have appealed to someone like Cellini, known for a violent character which repeatedly involved him in brawls, scandals and bloodshed. On the other hand, a Florentine contemporary, the historian Benedetto Varchi, proposed a gentler etymology: Florence, he said, was born on the flowery (*fiorite*) banks of the Arno and thus takes its name from flowers. In fact, the city's coat of arms has always included a lily. Botanists may insist that it is really an iris, but the fact remains that it is a flower.

What is certain is that Florence was founded by the Romans as a strategic outpost along the Via Cassia, at the confluence of the Mugnone and the Arno, and was called *Florentia*. In Caesar's time the Florentine *castrum* (camp), which controlled the consular routes from Rome, Faenza, Lucca and Pisa, was already an imposing city. Its fortifications, traces of which are still visible today, extended for two kilometres.

By the thirteenth century Florence had outgrown the original walls. New ones were built around the old, twice as long and crossing from the right to the left banks of the river. Two hundred years later a third system was built, extending for ten kilometres and encompassing a long portion of the Arno. At this time, according to Jean-Lucas Dubreton, author of *Daily Life in Florence at the Time of the Medici*, the city was a "perverse laboratory of politics" in which any pretext was enough to spark off bloody fighting between rival factions. Matteo Bandello, the famous sixteenth-century short-story writer, maintained that, "If all those who had been either chased from Florence or, lamentably, killed were gathered together, they would populate a city even larger than Florence."

Despite this climate of violence and an unwieldy bureaucracy, Dante's Florence flourished, thanks to the seven major *Arti* (guilds): the *Calimala* (importers of raw cloth to be transformed into precious materials), the *Lanaioli* (wool-workers), the *Setaioli* (silk-manufacturers), the *Pelliciai* (furriers), the *Medici e Speziali* (doctors and spice-merchants), the *Cambiatori* (bankers and money-changers) and the *Giudici e Notai* (judges and notaries), who meticulously administered and kept the financial records of the others.

The Ponte Vecchio, which spans the Arno at its narrowest point. It was probably built by the Romans, who wanted to extend the Via Cassia towards the north. Built of wood, on stone pilings, the bridge was destroyed by floods in 1117 and 1333. After the second time it was reconstructed in stone and widened to accommodate the now-famous shops along the sides. At first these housed a variety of trades, but since the end of the sixteenth century they have been the preserve of jewellers.

The Medici family gained its power through its involvement in trade and finance. From 1434, when Cosimo the Elder came to power, until the 1723 death of Cosimo III, Grand Duke of Tuscany, Florence's history was inextricably bound up with that of this great family, whose most illustrious representative was Lorenzo the Magnificent (1449-92). The fighting between factions came to an end only slowly; on two occasions the Medici were chased from Florence by a furious populace. Some family members fell victim to the daggers of conspirators or hired killers, while others were appointed cardinals or elected popes, and the legendary Catherine even became queen of France. The city of trade and finance became a capital of the arts. Even today, in spite of urbanization and industrialization, Florence's charm remains miraculously intact. The millions of visitors who flock there every year acknowledge that it represents the height of civilization and beauty.

Florence achieved this supremacy through adept entrepreneurship. But Siena got there first – one might even say Siena was born to it. The basis of its prosperity was a resource that Florence lacked: the silver of the Montieri mines. Other natural advantages include a particularly mild climate and the extremely pure air of the hills: the city is built on the heights that divide the Arbia and Elsa basins, whereas Florence is enclosed by a valley and is stifling in summer. Finally the Sienese, while Tuscan and therefore always ready for a dispute, live by a calmer and more tolerant philosophy than that of their compatriots.

Even in the fifteenth century, students were drawn to the old and prestigious university of Siena. Cultured men and women came to learn the most correct and harmonious Italian pronunciation, and diplomats gathered there to observe, from a discreet distance, politics in Florence and events in the nearby port of Leghorn. This amounted to so many foreigners that in the late sixteenth century travellers complained of being unable to learn Italian: they ended up speaking more with the English and Dutch than with the Sienese.

The city thus spawned an abundant foreign literature, inspiring writers as diverse as John Ruskin and Henry James. Charles Dickens described Siena as "a Venice without water"; Nathaniel Hawthorne saw the famous Piazza del Palio (also known as the Piazza del Campo) as a "seashell washed out by the sea of Time", and for an admiring Hippolyte Taine, Siena was "a city so well preserved that one could call it a Pompeii of the Middle Ages."

Siena's international vocation has persisted, a rare exception to the Italian provincialism that even today tends to separate the peninsula from the rest of Europe. Siena's traditions of hospitality and cultural exchange were born in the old *magioni* of the Knights Templar, where

Siena, laid out over three hills. The city walls, with a perimeter of approximately seven kilometres, have been enlarged many times over the centuries. The original inhabited nucleus of the city is today the Terziere di Città. Later came the Terziere di San Martino and, finally, Camollìa in the north-west. These terziere were in turn subdivided into contrade (quarters), which once numbered as many as fifty-nine.

Siena's Piazza del Campo, also known as the Piazza del Palio. Here, twice a year, riders representing the seventeen contrade compete in the frenzied, historic Palio horse-race. The name dates back to the days when the prize was a precious banner (pallium in Latin). In the foreground, the elegant Torre del Mangia. The nickname "Mangia" once was given to Giovanni di Duccio, a municipal employee in charge of striking the hour. Later, the name was transferred to the automaton that replaced him and which continued in this capacity until 1780.

The superb Piazza dei Cavalieri, in the historic centre of Pisa. The palace on the left belonged to the Knights of Saint Stephen (Cavalieri di Santo Stefano), an order founded by Grand Duke Cosimo I de' Medici to combat the pirates plaguing the Mediterranean coast in the second half of the sixteenth century. Next door is the church of Santo Stefano, discovered when two wings of the palace were renovated.

merchants and warriors mingled with pilgrims following the Via Francigena to Rome or the Holy Land, and in the palace of Prince Chigi, site of the renowned Accademia. Siena has kept these traditions alive, taking advantage of ever-developing means of communication. Today its colourful Palio, once just a popular local sport, is broadcast on television the world over.

Siena's destiny was played out along the Via Francigena, that great axis of European communication leading to the Baltic Sea in the north-east and Scotland in the north, and to the southern ports of Apulia, from which ships bearing Crusaders and pilgrims sailed for the Holy Land. Pisa's fortunes, on the other hand, centred on two Roman consular routes, the Via Aurelia and the Via Emilia Scauria. The first, virtually unchanged today, goes from Rome to Provence in France, following the upper Tyrrhenian coast. The second also leads out of Rome, but travels by the interior, joining up with the Via Francigena. If we add the Arno and especially the nearby sea, it would seem that Pisa's potential at the beginning was even greater than Siena's. Furthermore, Pisa built on its assets with investments that were as daring as they were rewarding.

An active naval base in Roman times, Pisa became one of the most important Mediterranean ports of call between the twelfth and thirteenth centuries. In less than two years, in 1015-16, Pisa had rid Sardinia of the Saracens and invaded Corsica. Allying itself with the Normans in the conquest of Sicily and profiting from the Crusades, it established commercial and military outposts in the Middle East and pushed west as far as the Balearic Isles, where its forces annihilated the Muslim armies. At the time of Frederick Barbarossa (who was crowned emperor in 1155), the Pisan flag flew over hundreds of fortresses in eastern Liguria. At the same time, feudal taxes paid by Naples, Salerno, Calabria and Sicily added to the already overflowing coffers of the Pisan treasury.

But Pisa's riches were ultimately responsible for the decline of its great maritime republic. Although its main rival, Amalfi, began to wane early in the eleventh century, Florence and Lucca applied pressure at Pisa's frontiers while Genoa, formerly an ally, attacked repeatedly and with increasing ferocity from the sea. In the epic battle of Meloria in 1284, Genoese ships destroyed forever the fleet – and final hopes – of Pisa.

Nonetheless, Pisa's golden age has bequeathed us noble institutions and splendid artworks: the Università della Sapienza, the Baptistery and, of course, the famous leaning tower which – like Florence's Palazzo Vecchio and Siena's Piazza del Palio – means Pisa to people worldwide. In the winter of 1989, the Italian authorities' decision to close the increasingly precarious tower to tourists made the front pages of newspapers around the world.

The Duomo of Pisa, the façade of which was designed by Rainaldo, a local architect. The three main doors, decorated with columns and pilasters, are surmounted by four rows of loggie. The cathedral was begun in 1064 and consecrated by Pope Gelasio II in 1118 – before its completion.

The Arno,
*dividing the centre of Florence.
In the foreground is the Ponte
alle Grazie; immediately behind
are the Ponte Vecchio, the Ponte
Santa Trinità and the Ponte
alla Carraia. On the left bank,
lit by the sun, is the Lungarno
(Quay) Torrigiani. On the
right bank, in the shade, is the
Lungarno Diaz. The Arno is
Italy's fourth-largest river,
flowing 248 kilometres from its
source at Monte Falterona in
the Tuscan-Emilian Apennines
to its delta on the Pisan coast.
Almost half of the river – 106
kilometres – is navigable.*

The Piazza and Church of the Holy Ghost (Santo Spirito), on the left bank of the Arno. Construction was begun in 1444 by Filippo Brunelleschi, who died two years later. The work was continued by other architects, whose unfortunate changes mar the original plans. The campanile, by Baccio d'Agnolo, was begun in 1503 and completed fourteen years later.

The Belvedere, or San Giorgio,
Fortress on the left bank of the Arno. Like the Piazzale Michelangelo, it is a spot from
which one can truly appreciate the splendid panorama of the city. The fortress was
constructed between 1590 and 1595 by Bernardo Buontalenti for Grand Duke
Ferdinando I; it is said that Giovanni de' Medici also participated in its design.
The star-shaped plan, with four major and two minor bastions, is considered one of the
most efficient military structures of its time, as it offered a full 360-degree defence.
At the centre is the Palazzetto del Belvedere, also the work of Buontalenti.

The church and campanile
of Saint Lawrence (San Lorenzo), rebuilt in the eleventh
century in Romanesque style atop an ancient basilica which
had been consecrated to Saint Ambrosius in 393. The
present structure, dating from 1419-60, was designed by
Brunelleschi and Antonio Manetti for the Medici. Right:
San Lorenzo facing the Duomo and Giotto's campanile,
in a panoramic view of the city.

The Boboli Gardens, which cover more than 40,000 square metres on a hilltop between the Pitti Palace, the Belvedere Fortress and the Roman Gate. It takes at least three hours to visit them properly. The gardens were commissioned by Eleanor of Toledo, daughter of Don Pedro, Viceroy of Naples, who married Cosimo I de' Medici in 1539. The original plans were drawn up by Niccolo Pericoli, better known as Tribolo, in 1550, the year of his death. Work was continued by Ammannati, Buontalenti and Alfonso Parigi the Younger.

The Carthusian
Monastery of Galluzzo,
in the luminous hills south
of Florence. It was founded
in 1341 by the Acciauoli,
an important Florentine
banking family, whose tombs
dating from the fourteenth
to sixteenth centuries are
housed in the underground
chapels. The monks' cells,
following the Florentine style,
are graced by an arcade
and a small garden.

The Piazza del Palio in
Siena. On the left is the famous Fonte Gaia, originally
decorated with reliefs by Jacopo della Quercia, which were
transferred to the Palazzo Pubblico and replaced in 1868
with reproductions by Tito Sarrocchi. The fountain's water
arrives via aqueduct from a spring twenty-five kilometres
away. Right: A panoramic view, showing the piazza just
behind and to the right of the glistening mass of the Duomo.

The Piazza del Palio and the apse of the Duomo. Construction of the Duomo began around the middle of the twelfth century, at the time of the rise of the free Communes. In 1196 a group of citizens formed an organization called the Opera di Santa Maria to further construction, which later continued under the management of the monks of San Galgano. The dome was erected in 1264, the apse three years later.

The façade of
the Duomo, completely in white
marble. The lower part, the
work of Giovanni Pisano, is
Romanesque with some Gothic
influence. The three portals are
surmounted by Gothic
tympana: the central one boasts
an architrave decorated with a
low relief by Tino da Camaino,
showing the story of Saint
Joachim and Saint Anne.
Many of the statues have been
replaced by copies, and the
originals moved to the Museo
dell'Opera to shelter them
from the effects of pollution.
The elaborate decoration of the
upper part is a superb example
of Flamboyant Gothic.

41

The church of
Santa Maria di Provenzano,
built in 1594 by architect-
sculptor Flaminio del Turco
according to the plans of
Damiano Schifardini, a
Carthusian monk. Inside are
four flags: three were taken in
battle by Sienese soldiers from
Turkish pirates in the
seventeenth and eighteenth
centuries, the fourth from the
Chinese during the Boxer
Rebellion of 1901.

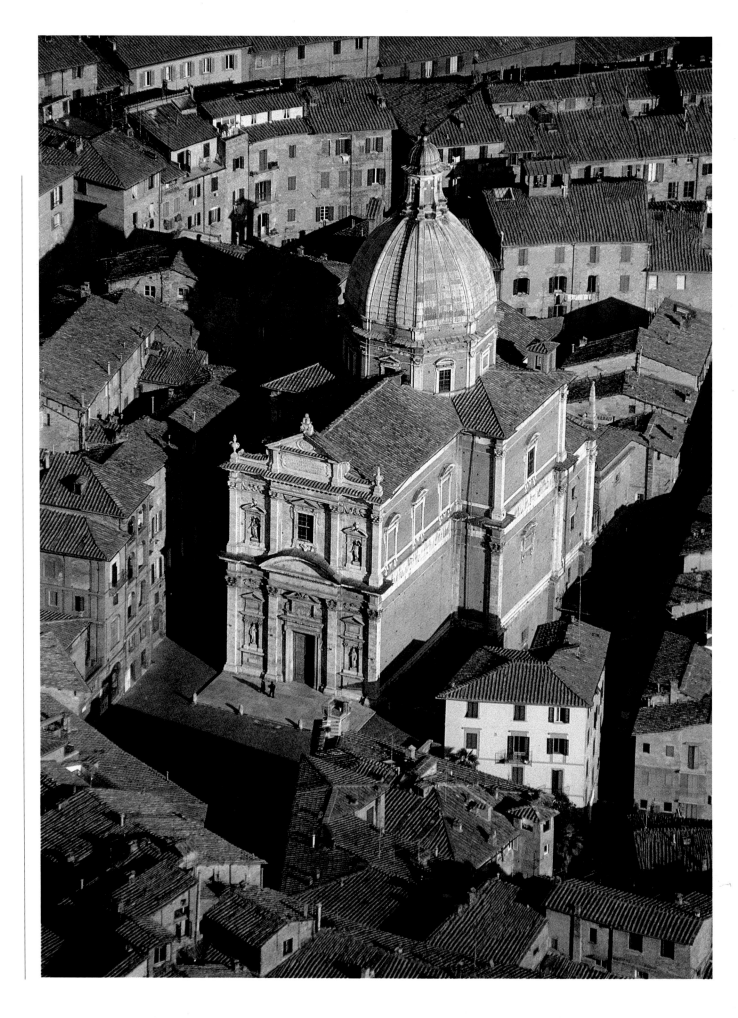

A portion of the imposing Siena city walls, the boundaries of the most unified, homogeneous and compactly beautiful Tuscan city. Repeatedly rebuilt as the city expanded, the irregular design of the seven-kilometre walls is due to Siena's Y-shaped layout, which is spread over three hills.

Siena, in the mists of dawn. For centuries the city's beauty has captivated artists and writers from all over the world. "Rich and pleasant" was how Sebastian Münster described Siena in his Voyage in Italy in 1573. He also admired the "comforts of living and the kindness of the citizens towards strangers". In 1784 Esther Lynch Piozzi wrote: "One little word would suffice to make me spend the rest of my life here." Such sentiments were echoed by many who took the Grand Tour, such as John Evelyn, Charles Dickens, Lady Blessington and John Ruskin.

P isa's famous leaning tower and the
apse of the Duomo bear witness to the power once attained by the city. Pisa grew up
along one of the three branches of the Arno delta, and its port was a major Roman
naval base at the time of the Second Punic War (218 BC). Six centuries later, Pisa
constructed a new port to the south of the city and, before establishing itself as a free
Commune, built an empire that began with the conquest of Sardinia and later
included Corsica and the Balearic Isles. Pisan merchants opened trading centres in
every Mediterranean port from North Africa to the Middle East.

The Piazza del Duomo, also called the Campo dei Miracoli (Field of Miracles). The tower's famous inclination is due to the unexpected settling of its foundations. It began to tilt at the beginning of its construction and now, more than seven centuries later, continues to keep the world in suspense. A chronicle dated 1292 mentions the fact that two architects, Giovanni di Nicola and Guido di Giovanni, were ordered to arrange two plumbs and a level in the interior to measure the tower's tilt every seven days.

P isa's Piazza
Santa Caterina. In the centre
of its harmonious garden stands
a statue in honour of Pietro
Leopoldo, Grand Duke of
Tuscany. Though officially
renamed Piazza of the Martyrs
of Liberty, the old name is still
used, due to the nearby Santa
Caterina church built by the
Dominicans between 1251
and 1300. The church has a
splendid marble façade in Pisan
style and a handsome brick
bell-tower.

The Palazzo dei Cavalieri di Santo
Stefano, built by Vasari in 1562 on the remains of the ancient Palazzo degli Anziani
(Palace of the Elders). A trace of the original structure is visible in the very high
blocked-up arch on the building's right side. In 1810 Napoleon chose this noble setting
for a prestigious university specializing in letters, philosophy, science and mathematics.
In front of the palace stands a statue of Cosimo I, with a fountain by Pietro
Francavilla. The external double staircase is a nineteenth-century addition.

The Lungarno Gambacorti, on the left bank of the Arno, along which a cortege marches annually to the bridge where the Mezzogiorno and Tramontana districts meet in the centuries-old Gioco del Ponte. The single white span of the Ponte di Mezzo joins the Borgo Stretto, the major architectural axis of the city, with the Corso Italia, a major shopping street. At the bottom of the photograph, the tiny church of Santa Maria della Spina, named for the piece of the Crown of Thorns which it housed. Built in 1323, the church was dismantled in 1871 and rebuilt a few metres further up the riverbank to protect it from water damage.

Pisa's Lungarno Pacinotti, on the right
bank of the Arno. Five centuries after Lorenzo the Magnificent came up with the idea
of the Gioco del Ponte as a means of channelling the once-deadly competitive energies
of the rival districts, this tumultuous contest still draws huge crowds of spectators.

The northern districts of Lucca. The piazza at the centre was once the site of a Roman amphitheatre built in the second century. The arena, some three metres below the current street level, was ringed with two tiers of arcades. The numerous houses built here between the seventeenth and eighteenth centuries were demolished in 1830 to make way for archaeological excavations.

THE
CITIES

E veryone agrees that Florence, Siena and Pisa are the three queens of Tuscany. Everyone, that is, except the Tuscans. The first to object would be the Florentines, the Sienese and the Pisans. Rather than take pride in such a characterization, each group would be insulted at the presumption that any other could share its pedestal. What's more, there are six other Tuscan county towns (Arezzo, Grosseto, Leghorn, Lucca, Massa Carrara and Pistoia), each taking great pride in *its* own history and traditions. To complicate matters, Tuscany is further divided into 278 – equally proud – communes. One might be tempted to smile at this cornucopia of competing claims, but there are certain questions of precedence over which no medieval knight would have hesitated to draw his sword.

It is undeniable that every Tuscan town and village harbours a distinct heritage so rich as to render arbitrary any attempt at classification. Lucca, for example, was the first city that could insist on the right to host a royal investiture. Founded by the Ligurians before the fifth century BC, Lucca was a rich Roman *municipium* in the first century AD, then capital successively of Tuscia under the Lombards, of the Marquisate of Tuscany during Charlemagne's time, and of the Napoleonic principality (the court of Elisa, the emperor's sister, was one of Europe's most brilliant). It was finally ceded to the House of Bourbon-Parma and Grand Duke Leopold II of Lorraine.

Lucca's great cultural, political and economic past has produced a fabulous array of palaces, churches, towers and fortifications, some dating as far back as from the Roman era. It is also a relatively large city (Lucca boasted a population of 100,000 at a time when Siena's was barely 60,000). But size was not the determining factor in Lucca's greatness, nor was it a prerequisite for the prominence of others. San Gimignano, for example, has just 7,000 inhabitants and can be visited in a half-day. Yet its beauty has attracted tourists from around the world for at least two

centuries. Admittedly, beautiful towns are hardly scarce in Tuscany. But San Gimignano seems to exist outside time, conserving intact an image of fourteenth-century life.

Though small, the town has a prestigious past. It grew up along the Via Francigena, its merchants establishing trading posts in Pisa, Marseilles, Lyons, Algiers, Gibraltar, London, Hamburg, Egypt and Palestine. They dealt in all types of merchandise, from *vernaccia*, the famous saffron wine, to sulphur (so precious in dyeing that it was even used as currency), as well as wool, silk, gold and leather. The tanneries of San Gimignano were so numerous and active that the town council had to enact a law to control pollution.

The walls of Lucca. What survives today is the third enclosure, built between 1504 and 1645 and later adapted to accommodate civilian traffic. This imposing defence system stretches more than four kilometres, with a base thirty metres thick and a height of twelve metres, and includes eleven bastions. Despite the city's stormy history, the walls were never put to the test.

And that was in the twelfth century! It was in this environment of extraordinary wealth that San Gimignano's celebrated tower-houses were built. They were symbols of the prestige of the principal families, each striving to go higher than the others. This competition became so intense that the governor was forced to limit the towers to a height of fifty-one metres so as not to surpass that of the Town Hall. But once again civil authority was treated to the disrespect of the powerful families. The Ardinghelli and the Salvucci erected two towers just under the limit, and informed the governor that the second tower had a base the same size as the summit of the first and that someday – one never knew – one might be put atop the other.

Cetona,
a picturesque hill town on the Siena-Chianciano road. Built by the Etruscans between Monte Cetona and the Astrone River, it was later conquered by the Romans, who made it into the popular vacation spot it remains today. In the 1970s the Roman jet set began to buy up land here, setting off a huge wave of real-estate speculation.

At that time there were sixty-five towers in San Gimignano, plus ten more along the fortifications. Today only eight remain, the others having been destroyed not by time but by civil war: the victory of one faction was sealed by the destruction of its rival's towers. These quarrels, culminating in the massacre of the Ardinghelli and Salvucci, ultimately led the town to surrender to Florence in 1352. Within a short time San Gimignano had lost all its riches, prestige and pride, and the very will to live.

It could be said that every Tuscan city, large or small, from the Middle Ages to the Renaissance ran the same risk of decline by way of internecine strife. What varied was their ability to react to the threats. Prato is an excellent example of the determination to survive. In the twelfth century, when a free Commune was constituted, the city was devastated by the battles of warring factions. Finally the exhausted adversaries submitted to the rule of Naples. Prato was then sold – for the insulting sum of 17,500 florins – to the government of Florence. Prato repeatedly rose up against Florence but was severely chastised each time and was finally sacked in 1512. Yet the great cultural prestige and economic might of this tormented city live on in the splendid Gothic churches of San Domenico and San Francesco, the Duomo, the basilica of Santa Maria degli Carceri and other monuments exhibiting the genius of such masters as Giovanni Pisano, Donatello and Giuliano da Sangallo. Daring and tenacious in industry and commerce (and still famous today for wool-working), Prato has risen again and again.

Similarly, Pistoia, a royal city during the Lombard era, succumbed to Florence only after centuries of war and conspiracy. There, monuments like the cathedral, San Bartolomeo, Sant'Antonio, San Giovanni, the Palazzo Pretorio and the Town Hall attest

San Gimignano, the medieval town overlooking the countryside of the Val d'Elsa. In the foreground, the walls that encircle the ancient fortress. Just behind is the cloister of the Collegiate Church of Santa Maria Assunta on the Piazza del Duomo, where stand the twin towers of the powerful Salvucci family. Their protracted and ferocious rivalry with the Ardinghelli brought about the ruin of the entire town. To the right of the church, the tower of the Town Hall and, behind, the tower called La Rognosa (The Mangy One), named after a tight-fisted chief magistrate.

today to a rich local heritage. And so it is with Monteriggioni, a town still ringed by ancient fortifications. Its strategic position as a Sienese military outpost on Florence's borders condemned Monteriggioni to a fate of siege and pillage at the hands of one rival or another, yet fourteen towers still rise miraculously from its walls. Many other places, such as Certaldo, Castiglion Fiorentino, Montepulciano and Pescia, also contain testimonies of glorious pasts, often amazingly intact, in spite of real-estate predators and neglectful municipal councils.

Some of Tuscany's towns are indelibly marked by their Etruscan origins, though the legacy of succeeding civilizations – particularly that of the conquering Romans – makes this difficult to recognize. Arezzo is no longer a great city, but it preserves a regal grace. During the Etruscan era it belonged to a confederation of twelve city-states whose rulers, called *Lucumone*, held supreme political power as well as religious authority. Some 700 metres of its ancient city walls, which guarded against barbarian invasions until the decline of the Roman Empire, still stand.

Equally rich and powerful, Volterra, the Etruscan Velathri, also was part of the confederation. There archaeologists have found traces of a Villanovian civilization that predated the Etruscans and was amongst the most advanced of prehistoric times. Since that distant age Volterra has been famous for alabaster, which is still extracted from the region's seemingly inexhaustible quarries. In Cortona, spread over the steep slopes of Monte Sant'Egidio, Etruscan origins also are recognizable – in the walls, made of massive rectangular blocks, that still surround parts of the town. As in Arezzo and Volterra, the cramped architecture of the Middle Ages was superimposed onto the early Etruscan structures. Cortona's medieval style is especially noteworthy. The houses have remarkable façades, their upper storeys overhanging the very narrow streets and resting on robust wooden supports. Cortona is a city of antique dealers; its annual trade fair is renowned. But more, it is a city of silence and memory. From the Belvedere one can look out on the enchanting Valdichiana, at the heart of a constellation of Tuscan and Umbrian art centres – Florence, Siena, Assisi, Gubbio, Perugia and Città di Castello – all within easy reach. This is the stuff that dreams are made of – as well as nightmares. Legend has it that every year, during the night of 24 June, one can hear the wailing of Consul Gaius Flaminius' 5,000 legionnaires, who were massacred on that date in 217 BC by Hannibal's troops.

Castiglion Fiorentino, on the Arezzo-Cortona road. This town has been renamed a number of times by its successive conquerors. It was Aretino, then Perugino before becoming Fiorentino in 1384. Since the distant past it has been a flourishing trade centre, attracting entrepreneurs from all over the Valdichiana. Traces of the medieval walls still exist, as do the fourteenth- and fifteenth-century towers.

Another superb
panorama of San Gimignano.
Abelardo, Bishop of Volterra,
was posted here by King
Hugues of Provence to serve
as spiritual guide for the few
inhabitants and to maintain
order. The site was actually
of great strategic importance,
overlooking the road that led
from the capital of the Italic
kingdom, then located at Pavia,
to Rome and to the ports
of Puglia, from which boats
carrying pilgrims or Crusaders
set sail for the Holy Land. This
position on the Via Francigena
favoured the development
of the city, which became one
of the richest and most powerful
in central Italy.

A panoramic view of Lucca. Towards the bottom of the foreground is the tip of the San Donato bastion in the north-west part of the city walls. To the left is the Santa Croce bastion and, to the right, that of San Paolino. At the beginning of the nineteenth century, the vast terreplein was transformed into a tree-lined ring, creating an appealing area in which to stroll. Above: the historic city centre.

Lucca's
Church of San Frediano
(Saint Frigidian). Built between
1112 and 1147 in the shelter
of the town's first fortifications,
its campanile was, in both form
and function, more military
than religious. Adding to
the sense of split-personality,
the church's entrance and
façade have been moved from
one side of the building to the
other; they were originally beside
the bell-tower. Directly above is
the picturesque Piazza
dell'Anfiteatro.

Lucca's Duomo, founded in the sixth century and reconstructed many times. The surviving version of the façade is asymmetrical. The style is solemnly Roman, with three tiers of arcades above the great triple-arched porch. An extraordinary richness is provided by the variety of forms and materials: the multi-coloured marble, the alternately straight or twisted columns

Two views of Lucca's aqueduct. It was built by the architect Lorenzo Nottolini during the reign of Marie Louise of Bourbon, between 1820 and 1830. The aqueduct carries water to Lucca from a spring at Guamo, a hamlet in Capannori, about twelve kilometres to the east. Other Nottolini works in Lucca include an imposing grand staircase which leads to the first floor of the national art gallery, the Pinacoteca Nazionale.

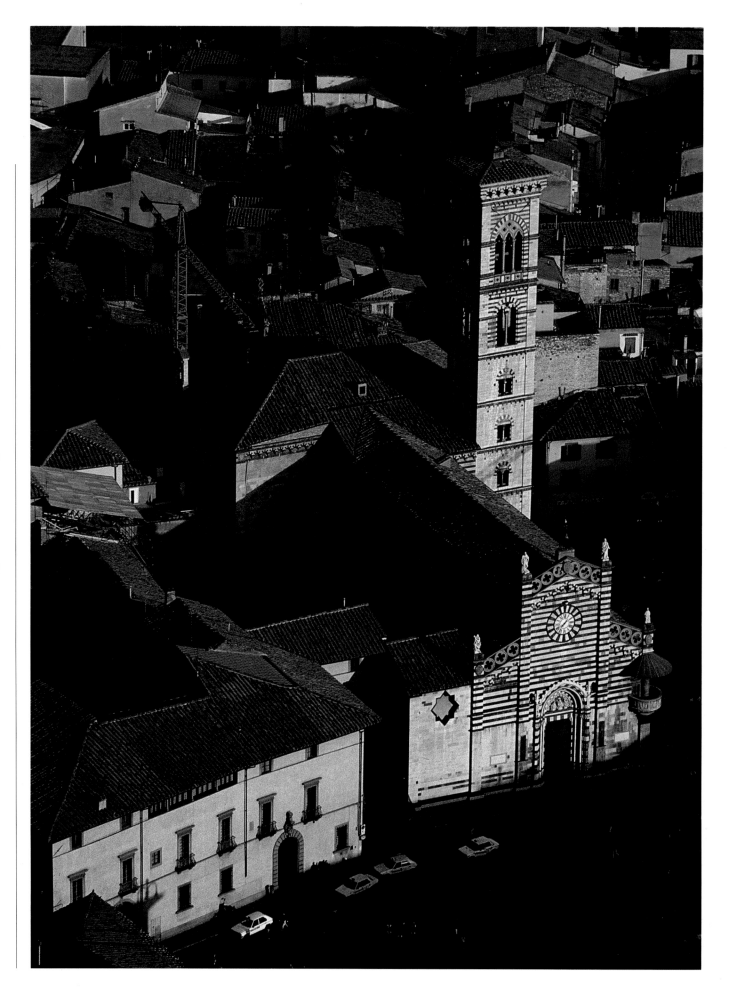

The Duomo of Prato was built in its current form in 1211 by Guidetto da Como atop the remains of the church of Santo Stefano, which dated from the ninth century. In the fourteenth century the building was enlarged by a vast transept with five ogival chapels. The church is renowned for its relic of the Holy Sash, which is conserved in a richly frescoed chapel. The sash, used for attaching sacerdotal vestments, is said to have been given by the Virgin Mary to Saint Thomas, who gave it to a priest. The sash was included in the dowry of the priest's great-niece whose husband, Michele Dagomari, gave it to the city after surviving a turbulent sea crossing.

Prato's Emperor's Castle, built between
1237 and 1248 on the orders of Frederick II. Much earlier, another fortress, residence
of the Counts of Prato, occupied this site. The simple yet powerful design of Frederick's
castle recalls other Swabian castles in Puglia and Sicily. The square plan has towers
at each corner and along the perimeter walls; the sentry walk affords
a splendid view over the city.

The Duomo of Pistoia,
which also appears at the centre of the view on the right, was
constructed in the fifth century and rebuilt in the thirteenth.
The entry boasts an elegant portico. The bell-tower was
originally a Lombard watchtower; the three upper storeys
were added at the end of the thirteenth century. Facing it is
the grandiose octagonal Baptistery, constructed in 1338 by
Cellino di Nese after the design of Andrea Pisano.

Monteriggioni, one of the most picturesque towns in Tuscany. Dante described it as "completely enclosed within its round circle". Located on a small hill between Florence and Siena, the town was founded by the Sienese in 1203 as a military outpost. It passed from one city to the other in the course of a struggle that began soon after the year 1000 and ended five centuries later with Siena's surrender to Florence. The first walls, which dated from 1213, were reinforced between 1260 and 1270. Fourteen towers punctuate the sentry walk. The "circle" is barely 570 metres long.

Cortona, enclosed within the ancient walls that climb the steep slopes of Sant'Egidio to the Fortress of Girifalco. The original urban design was Etrusco-Roman, with the two principal streets crossing in the centre of town. There stand the Palazzo Communale or Town Hall, and the Palazzo Pretorio. The Duomo is further to the north, facing the plain. Above: the town centre, with the distinctive sky-blue cupola of the Church of Saint Philip.

73

Arezzo, where the superb Romanesque
church of Santa Maria recalls the original medieval nucleus of the city. The bell-tower
is called "the Hundred Mouths" after the five tiers of paired windows that decorate each
of its four walls. Following the Via della Seteria one emerges onto the Piazza Grande,
bordered by the Law Courts and the Palazzo della Fraternità dei Laici (Palace of the
Lay Brotherhood). One side of the piazza (that shown in full sun) is dominated by
the magnificent Palazzo delle Logge, designed by Giorgio Vasari. In the arcades,
medieval shops still do business.

In the southern part of the city,
not far from the railway station, are the remains of a Roman amphitheatre.
The structure dates from the end of the first century and the beginning of the second.
An ellipse 121 metres long and 63 metres wide, the amphitheatre contained two tiers
of stands and could hold approximately 8,000 people. Already prominent during
the Etruscan era, Arezzo was an important military base under the Romans, due
to its strategic location on the Via Cassia.

Volterra. In the foreground
stands the ship-like fortress with its two main sections: the
trapezoidal Rocca Vecchia and, to the left, the Rocca Nuova.
The Rocca Vecchia, called "The Female", is fourteenth
century; the Nuova, "The Male", was commissioned by
Lorenzo the Magnificent around 1472. Above: the Duomo
and the Baptistery, crowned by an octagonal cupola. To the
left, the bell-tower, pierced by three sets of double windows.

Collodi, between Montecatini and Pisa, is known for having furnished the nom de plume of Carlo Lorenzini, author of Pinocchio. In the foreground is the impressive Villa Garzoni, built in 1600 atop the remains of a medieval castle. In the adjacent park, tourists can admire a monument showing Pinocchio and the Blue Fairy, a work by Emilio Greco.

The ancient town of Pitigliano clings to a spur of tufa that rises above the ravines of Meleta, Leuta and Prochio. The houses, built one against another, provided an imposing wall which complemented a natural defence system. Towards the end of the thirteenth century, the town passed from the Aldobrandeschi, a noble Roman family, to the Orsini, who made it a bishopric and capital of their county. In addition to its powerful defences, the Orsini also gave the town some of the Renaissance architecture that gracefully mixed with the medieval framework. Antonio da Sangallo the Younger, briefly chief architect of Saint Peter's Basilica in Rome, worked here between 1543 and 1545.

Montepulciano, on a hill between Valdichiana and the Valle dell'Orcia, is a noble town that has preserved some superb late-Renaissance monuments. In the upper left appears the Duomo, built between 1592 and 1630 on the remains of an ancient church whose elegant fifteenth-century bell-tower has survived. Near the cathedral, at the centre of the piazza, is the Town Hall, dating from the second half of the fourteenth century.

Pienza, one of Tuscany's most famous
art cities, began life as a modest medieval castle called Corsignano. After becoming
the property of the Abbey of Monte Amiata, it passed to the Piccolomini, a noble
Sienese family. A Piccolomini, Enea Silvio (born here in 1405 and proclaimed Pope
Pius II in 1458) decided to transform the small town into an ideal city, renaming it
Pienza. To the right is the cathedral, designed by Bernardo Rossellino and erected
between 1459 and 1462. In the centre, the majestic gallery and gardens
of the Piccolomini Palace.

P escia, the most important hub of Valdinievole, between Lucca and Pistoia. In the past this was a flourishing centre of printing, leather-tanning and the cultivation of mulberry trees for the silk industry. More recently Pescia has specialized in horticulture – the photograph shows its vast greenhouses – and is considered a serious rival to horticulturally preeminent San Remo, on the Ligurian Riviera. Pescia has extended on both sides of the river which bears the same name.

T*he environs of Florence, renowned for the charm of the countryside as well as for myriad landmarks of historical and artistic importance. In the foreground is the Villa Il Tondo, which overlooks a bend of the Via di San Domenico. The restored southern façade of the villa shows a typical symmetry and elevated central portion.*

THE

HILLS

A gentle slope striped with grapevines. A field of golden grain, and green pastures soft as carpets. The rich earth recently turned, the furrows dark and damp. Olive trees with glistening leaves and, higher up, between the cypresses, a rustic farm or elegant nobleman's villa.

This is the classic scenery of the Tuscan hills – or, it could be said, of Tuscany in general, as the hills account for two-thirds of the region. The term "Tuscan hills" is necessarily generic, since it is difficult to establish just where the hills begin and the mountains end between the Apennines to the north and the *colline* further south. The buildings that dot this tranquil landscape are distinguished by their functions, civil or religious: peasant houses and villas on the one hand, churches and monasteries on the other. An exact count of houses, even one limited to the larger and more prestigious, is virtually impossible. In Florence alone, the definitive Italian Touring Club guide mentions sixteen villas, with another 105 in the immediate environs. For the overall region there are more than a thousand. Similarly abundant are the abbeys, convents, hermitages and small roadside chapels.

Jean-Lucas Dubreton wrote that the life of the Medici-era Florentine revolved around three fixtures: his house in town, the shop in which he worked, and his country villa or farm – in Mugello, for instance, the region above the Sieve Valley. Many such wool- or silk-manufacturers and their families made peaceful country homes in remodelled castles. There were more than 800 of these stone-and-lime residences, known pretentiously as *palazzi*, within a thirty-kilometre radius of Florence. With such homes, the once-rustic countryside began to put on airs. Sometimes a wing simply was added to a farmhouse. Others built grand country villas from scratch, specially designed to represent the owner's wealth and to offer him a place of escape. Still, while on his country estate the master took an active interest in the progress of the harvest and the well-being of the peasants – as in the happy days celebrated by Horace.

Cosimo de' Medici had a villa built by Michelozzo in 1458 at Fiesole, on a site so enjoyable he called it *Belcanto*, to mean "lovely place". Here Lorenzo the Magnificent later gathered the writers and artists of his court, such as Poliziano, Pico della Mirandola and Cristoforo Landino – a group of noble friends, appreciated for their brilliant minds and refined tastes, who shared a passion for living life to the fullest. Can it be mere coincidence that, 110 years earlier, Boccaccio had imagined the ten youths of *The Decameron* fleeing plague-ridden Florence to relate their delightfully naughty tales in a villa at Fiesole?

But when one speaks of Tuscany's hills and villas it is Chianti that springs to mind. Chianti has become a universally recognized name through its wine, one of the world's most famous.

The Church of San Paolo della Croce, built a century ago by the Passionisti Order adjoining their convent. Located near the often-deafening autoroute, this place is an unexpected haven of solitude and silence.

The town of Artimino, in the environs of Florence. A fortified castle during the Middle Ages, constructed atop Etruscan and Roman ruins, the entrance gate of the first watchtower and a few sections of the old walls still stand. Nearby is one of the most beautiful Medici villas, La Ferdinanda, built by Ferdinando I as a hunting pavilion. The project, begun in 1594, was supervised by Bernardo Buontalenti.

The wine has been so widely imitated that one is surprised to discover Chianti is actually tiny, covering no more than 300 square kilometres of hills between the Arno basin south of Florence and the Ombrone basin north of Siena. Sir Harold Acton, the British author who has adopted Florence as his home, said that if all the wine sold as Chianti actually came from Chianti, the vineyards would have to cover an area equivalent to the steppes of Central Asia.

Chianti is indeed small, but it is rich in grape varieties – the Sangiovato and Canaiolo reds, the Trebbiano and Malvasia whites, to name just a few. The traveller who sets out to discover Chianti will find a myriad different wines whose labels proudly bear the coats-of-arms or names of towns, villages and noble families, like Radda, Barberino and Tavernelle. Chianti is also rich in architecture. Its most famous castle is that of the Ricasoli family, at Brolio near Gaiole. The vast audience chamber, as solemn as a church, is hung on all sides with banners tattered by the winds of a thousand battles in which the Ricasoli fought. The castle has existed at least since Charlemagne's time, and the Ricasoli have lived there since the twelfth century. Its walls have been assaulted successively by lances and swords, crossbows, arquebuses and bombards, rifles, machine guns and bazookas. The most recent shots were fired there in 1944 by the British Eighth Army, when the castle was once again cast in the role of strategic outpost. And as in the past, the wine continued to age peacefully in large oak casks in the cellars. "All the wars have passed by here," says the Baron Ricasoli. "However, we have never lost the desire to sing and drink."

To Tuscans, their region's main artery is the wine route that runs through Chianti. But also important is Tuscany's "water route", which leads to numerous thermal spas. The queen of these is Montecatini, west of Florence and halfway between Pistoia and Lucca. Elsewhere in Tuscany, the traveller tends to feel, as Stendhal said, that he has stepped into the sixteenth century. But the thermal style, of which Montecatini is typical, takes its inspiration from the avant-garde of the early twentieth century, making concessions to the grandiose while maintaining a certain elegance. Montecatini's sulphur springs were famous in ancient times and are mentioned in a thirteenth-century medical text, *De Balneorum Italiae proprietatibus* (*Concerning the Properties of Thermal Waters in Italy*), which vaunted their virtues in the treatment of liver ailments. The first installations were constructed shortly thereafter, on the initiative of the city of Florence. At the end of the sixteenth century the entire establishment became the private property of the Medici, an indication of how profitable the spas had become. But major development in the modern sense did not occur until two centuries later, under the

The former farm buildings of the Fattoria dell'Amorosa at Sinalunga, in the heart of the Valdichiana, now house one of Tuscany's most celebrated restaurants. Sinalunga became the town's name in 1864, when the original name, Asina-lunga (which means "the long she-ass"), was deemed undignified. The hamlet was once reportedly famous throughout the region for possessing a she-ass longer than any other ever seen. It was at Sinalunga, in 1867, that Giuseppe Garibaldi was arrested as he attempted to rejoin the Roman insurgents.

The Carthusian monastery at Farneta, a few kilometres outside Lucca via the Pietrasanta road. The monastery was constructed in the fourteenth century, when the city was alternately governed by various lords. Over the centuries, the monastery grew with the increasing importance of the Benedictine Order. At the centre is a square cloister surrounded by a harmonious arcade. In the church is preserved a gilded silver reliquary of the True Cross, a precious example of seventh-century Byzantine art.

enlightened government of the Grand Dukes of Lorraine, who were also responsible for clearing the land and draining the marshes.

Farms, villas, castles, vineyards, olive groves, thermal spas – these are the non-religious components of the Tuscan hills. One might even call them "pagan", since behind these landmarks one can discern the hand of Renaissance Man, sole master on Earth and conscious of being so, intent on enjoying life as long as it lasted. In the words of Lorenzo the Magnificent: "Chi vuol esser lieto sia, del doman non c'è certezza." ("Let him who wishes to rejoice do so, because there is no certainty in tomorrow.")

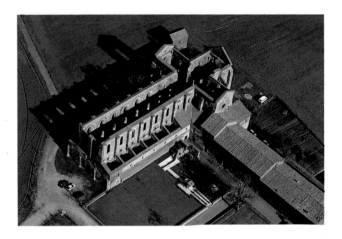

Yet Renaissance Man was born in the misery and fear of the Middle Ages, when the only hope of salvation lay in commending oneself to Christ, the Virgin Mary and all the saints of the Christian Olympus. Thus religion forged the other aspect of the Tuscan hills, the expressions of a mystical and severe yet gentle faith. Examples are found everywhere, from a minuscule chapel whose naive frescoes have been erased by time to grandiose abbeys rich in artworks, precious books and manuscripts.

One of the most notable abbeys is San Salvatore, which clings to the slopes of Monte Amiata. Founded by Ratchis the Lombard in 743, this monastery has been administered over the years by the Benedictines, the Camaldoletians and the Cistercians. Once one of the richest in Tuscany, it remains today one of the most beautiful. The abbey of Farneta, near Cortona, has a history dating back more than a thousand years. Even more grandiose is the imposing Monte Oliveto Maggiore, overlooking the Sienese Hills; founded at the beginning of the fourteenth century, it contains magnificent frescoes by Sodoma and Luca Signorelli. San Galgano, one of the great masterpieces of the Cistercian-Gothic style, was built at the end of the twelfth century by Guido Guidotti, a nobleman and brilliant knight who became a hermit; its land once extended all the way to Grosseto. Sant'Antimo, on a hill between the Asso and Ombrone rivers, has origins even older and more illustrious: it was founded by Charlemagne, and its abbot was one of the most powerful Sienese feudal landlords of the Middle Ages. Then there are the ruins of San Rabano, erected by the Benedictines on the eve of the millennium and turned over to the Knights of the Military Order of Saint John of Jerusalem. Not to mention the abbeys of Torri, San Savinio and Spineta.

Yet even as it bows before the ultimate authority of Christianity, Tuscany exerts its proud sense of self. In Tuscany, Christianity was obliged to learn to speak Tuscan. And images of the Virgin Mary tend to smile with the grace of Venus Urania, rather than expressing the anguish of the Mother of God.

Remains of the Abbey of San Galgano, at the south-west edge of the Sienese province. The abbey developed from 1224 to 1288 on the site of a hermitage to which Galgano Guidotti, a brilliant young knight, retired after having driven his sword into a rock in a renunciation of violence. Like his contemporary, Francis of Assisi, Galgano was profoundly attached to Nature; legend holds that he spoke with birds and was watched over by wolves. Four years after his death, in 1185, Pope Lucius III made him a saint and ordered a chapel constructed on the spot where he had lived and was buried. The abbey was later constructed nearby.

The hills on the south-east periphery of
Florence. Above, to the right, is the Torre del Gallo (the Rooster's Tower). During
the Middle Ages this was one of the city's most important watchtowers, surveying
the roads leading from Siena.

O ne hill beyond another in a rarified light
that calls to mind an old Chinese print. We are in the Sienese countryside, having
crossed the Via Francigena which, in the eighteenth century, bore the traffic of
the Grand Tour just as, 700 years earlier, it was travelled by Crusaders, merchants
and pilgrims. The eighteenth-century traveller using his own carriage covered about
fifty-seven kilometres per day; the coaches which changed horses en route
could log up to 157 kilometres.

A panoramic view of Fiesole. Atop the hill to the left is the campanile of the fourteenth-century Church of San Francesco, originally an oratory of the neighbouring convent of Florentine Romites. Not far below, in the centre of the photograph, is the tower of the Palazzo Comunale. Fiesole, an Etruscan town, has preserved magnificent examples of its origins (long sections of the Etruscan walls still stand) and of the later Roman conquest. From the latter period, archaeologists have unearthed an amphitheatre, baths and remains of some civil and religious buildings.

The hills that encircle Florence are dotted with churches and villas, superb even when they are not authentic. The Torre del Gallo was reconstructed at the beginning of this century, according to contemporary fashion, atop medieval ruins which already had been restored on numerous occasions. It was rebuilt by an antiques dealer as a showcase for his collections.

The hill of Arcetri south of Florence is the site of the Astrophysical Observatory. It was here, in the Villa Il Gioiello (the Jewel), that Galileo died in 1642. After the first condemnation of the Holy Office, in 1616, he had retired here, already in poor health, to be near his beloved daughter Virginia, who lived in a nearby convent as Sister Mary Celeste. She died prematurely in 1634, a year after the Holy Office's second condemnation of her father's theories.

The landscape of the Tuscan hills is dominated by medieval and Renaissance architecture, but it also boasts interesting specimens of later styles. This villa, reached by a long alley that cuts through the fields and ends in a harmonious garden, dates from the eighteenth century, the era of the Grand Dukes. The neo-Classical façade has lost its symmetry through the attachment of the farm buildings on the left.

I n the hills near Lucca, a small farm
echoes – on a more modest scale – the proportions of medieval castle architecture:
the principal structure dominates the lesser buildings. Here the master's house
has been surrounded by those of his sons, built according to a strict hierarchy. Many
such properties, often uninhabited, have become the objects of intense real-estate
speculation as a desire to "return to Nature" has driven the inhabitants
of European cities to seek refuge in the countryside.

D*ark green,
pale green, white, lavender:
the Tuscan landscape is
characterized by these chance
tonal variations. Over the
centuries this landscape has
been profoundly altered,
as cultivation has spread
away from the immediate
surroundings of the castle, to
which it had been restricted for
reasons of security during the
tumultuous Middle Ages.*

A vineyard in Chianti. Besides the Sangioveto, the principal Chianti grapes are the Canaiolo black and the Malvasia and Trebbiano whites which, when combined, give the ruby-red Chianti its faint perfume of violets. The denomination of Chianti includes wine from such neighbouring regions as Greve, Val d'Elsa, Val di Pesa, Poggibonsi, San Casciano Verberino and Castelnuovo Berardenga.

A *road winds towards the summit of a hill between cypress trees, which contribute yet another shade of green. Despite all man's "progress", much of the Tuscan landscape remains virtually intact. A setting like this shows the inspiration behind the presepi or crèches made in the thirteenth century, with their processions of knights and shepherds making their way to the manger in Bethlehem.*

Chianti's stone structures have a look all
their own, in the old churches, castles, farms and scattered rural houses. The original
architecture of this castle has been profoundly altered as military requirements gave
way to civilian amenities. The inner courtyard, for example, has been hidden beneath
a roof, while the sentry walk around the walls has simply disappeared. An elegant
portico has been added to the façade, where the drawbridge most likely used to be.
As for the moat, no trace remains.

The colourful Chianti hills, between
the basins of the Arno, south of Florence, and the Ombrone, north of Siena. The soil
is made up of marly limestone, sand and clayey shale. More than half the area is
covered by woods — oak, chestnut, holm oak and pine. The other half is cultivated,
the vineyards and olive groves representing the oldest and still most important
regional source of wealth.

One castle detail that might escape
the foreign visitor indicates to which political party the owner belonged. Tuscan cities
and towns were divided between the Guelphs, loyal to the pope, and the Ghibellines,
followers of the emperor. If the crenellations crowning the fortifications are square, as
above, the castle was Guelph; a two-pointed style was favoured by the Ghibellines.

Famous the world over for the exquisite
wine it has produced since ancient times, Chianti is in fact a tiny territory, covering
just 300 square kilometres. The author Sir Harold Acton, British by birth but
Florentine by adoption, maintained that if all the wine sold as Chianti were actually
produced here, the region would have to be as large as the steppes of Central Asia.

A typical farm in Chianti. The region's economy, as far back as the Roman era, has largely depended on the production of wine, for which the climate and soil are especially favourable. The Sangioveto black is the father of the noble Tuscan grapes; the Romagnols on the other side of the Apennines claim it comes from their Sangiovese.

Another example of rural Tuscan
architecture in the midst of tilled fields. The house of the Renaissance-era proprietor,
who came here from the city for rest and relaxation (as well as to oversee his rural
affairs), had to remain distinct from the dwellings of the peasants and other workers
of the domain. The master's villa was therefore larger and higher, even if built in two
storeys like more modest houses. The access staircase here is on the outside and
characterized by a certain solemnity, to underline the distance between
those who serve and those who are served.

A few kilometres from Siena, on the
Arezzo road, stands the imposing Castello delle Quattro Torri (Castle of Four Towers).
It was built between the fourteenth and fifteenth centuries according to a square plan
similar to the contemporary castle of the Estes in Ferrara. The windows of the lower
storeys are very narrow, the larger openings reserved for the upper,
less vulnerable, floors.

The splendid castle of Brolio, in the heart of the Chianti region. All the wars have passed by here, including the Second World War, when the British Eighth Army stormed the noble walls that had withstood so many other assaults over the past thousand years. Documents concerning the castle date back to the ninth century; the property has belonged to the Ricasoli family since 1141. The current Baron Ricasoli lives here and, like his forebears, oversees production of the famous Brolio wine, still made and aged in the same majestic cellars.

An autumn day in the Sienese countryside.
The undulating furroughs of earth, punctuated by a swath of brightly coloured woods,
compose a scene worthy of a great landscape painter.

In the landscape of Chianti, the geometry
of man's cultivations is still interrupted by irregular shapes imposed by the natural
physical characteristics of the land. The movement of the line and the varied palette
of colours are a delight to the eye.

The mention of Tuscany often evokes an image of olive groves bordered by dark cypresses, eternal guardians of a landscape that even intensive exploitation has not managed to destroy. Chianti's image, symbolized by grape and olive, is also rolling wooded hills and mountains, which mark the region's somewhat vague north-east boundaries.

The Tuscan landscape, and especially
that of Chianti, is dotted with white flocks which still make the seasonal journey
between mountain pastures and those on the Tyrrhenian coast. From these
sheep comes the famous pecorino, a delicate cheese with a hint of sweetness that
comes from the particular richness and variety of the forage.

The castle of Montecchio, between Arezzo
and Cortona, still surrounded by the walls which have stood for more than
a millennium. The castle belonged successively to the Guisponi family of Arezzo,
the Marchesi di Santa Maria, the Republic of Arezzo, and to Florence, which ceded it to
the Englishman John Hawkwood, a condottiere or independent military leader.
(Hawkwood's name proved too difficult for the Italians, who called him Giovanni
Acuto.) Today all that remains of the interior palace are its foundations.

J ust outside Siena sits the imposing
fortress-hermitage of Lecceta, in the heart of a dense forest. One of Europe's oldest
hermitages, it was founded by a few Augustinian monks in the fifth century and was
enlarged and fortified over the years. The church was rebuilt in 1317 after being
destroyed by fire, and was renovated in the seventeenth century. One cloister dates
from the thirteenth century and has column-lined arcades. The other, from the fifteenth
century, boasts brick pilasters. This complex is now in a state of almost total abandon.

The Abbey of Monte Oliveto Maggiore,
in the Arbia Valley south of Siena. This vast monastery grew up around a simple
hermitage to which, in 1310, Bernardo Giovanni Tolomei, a brilliant law professor
and scion of one of Siena's richest and most famous families, withdrew to a life
of prayer and penitence. Three years later he founded the Olivetan Order, which was
recognized by the Bishop of Arezzo in 1319 and submitted to Benedictine rule;
work on the church and monastery began the following year. The abbey houses
numerous artworks and a valuable library.

The Church of San Leonardo at Artimino, a settlement whose roots date back to Etruscan times. It is believed that the church was founded by Countess Matilda di Canossa in 1107. The Romanesque plan has been brought back to light through careful restoration following a disastrous renovation at the start of the eighteenth century. The restoration discovered that Etruscan urns had been used as construction material.

The thermal springs at Saturnia, between
Grosseto and Lake Bolsena. Tuscany, known for its wine, is also famous for its water,
with numerous springs exploited since Antiquity. The sulphur waters of Saturnia,
whose temperature is a constant 37 degrees Centigrade, are particularly recommended
for those suffering from rheumatism, respiratory ailments or gastric afflictions.
Nearby is the town of Saturnia, still enclosed by ancient walls from a settlement which
pre-dated the Etruscans. Legend holds that this was the first town of the Italic peoples,
founded by the god Saturn who, dethroned by Zeus, sought refuge here
between Tuscany and Latium.

One of the most elegant spas in thermal Tuscany: Montecatini Terme, between Pistoia and Lucca. The springs, recommended even in ancient times for liver ailments, became the property of the Medici in 1583. In the second half of the eighteenth century Grand Duke Pietro Leopoldo turned them over to the Benedictines of Florence, under whose skillful management the spa began to attract many clients. Currently eight springs are exploited, each with its own therapeutic properties.

The north-west limits of Tuscany, between the Tyrrhenian coast, Liguria and Emilia, where the Apuan Alps rise. (Their name comes from the ancient Apuan Ligurians, a people who settled in this area before the Roman conquest). It is springtime, the valleys are already green, while the mountain peaks are still covered with snow. The Apuan chain stretches for sixty kilometres, parallel to the coast.

THE
MOUNTAINS

In the nineteenth century, travellers on the Grand Tour left the boat at Genoa, having sailed in from Spain or France, and crossed into Tuscany from Liguria. The road to Leghorn, Henry James said, was the most beautiful in Italy and got better the slower it was taken. On setting foot in Tuscany, one is confronted by high, severe mountains which seem like a prolongation of the great chain of the Alps. These are the Apuan Alps and, although similar in name, height and very hard rock, they are a chain apart.

The Apuan Alps have been famous since ancient times for their inexhaustible marble quarries, whose treasures have been prized by sculptors and builders for centuries: the pure Statuario, so white that from a distance its quarries look like ice; the pale and the dark Bardiglio, between sky blue and turquoise; the yellow-and-black Paonazzo; the green Cipollino; the violet and the orange Breccia; the grey-veined Arabescato.

The Romans waged an intense war against the Apuans to take over their territory and not simply for strategic reasons – for the quarries as well. At the end of the first century BC when the Emperor Augustus rebuilt Rome in splendid marble (the city was once largely brick), the stonemasons went to the Apuans for their stock. Removing the marble was a herculean task, and slaves were brought in from all over the Empire. Thousands of men paid with their lives for the glory of Rome and the Caesars, and much marble was lost during the difficult extraction process. Quarry masters inserted pegs of soft wood into fissures and wet them so the pegs swelled and split the rock according to a precise design. The blocks were then transported to the port of Luni on rollers coated with soap; each load required fifty pairs of oxen. Once at Luni, the monoliths were loaded onto enormous flat-bottomed barges and towed by galleys down the Tyrrhenian coast to the mouth of the Tiber and on to Rome. On average, only a third of the shipments arrived at their final destination; the others were sunk by storms at sea. The power of the marble capital, Luni, waned for geological reasons: sediment blocked the port and land took the place of the sea. Today little remains of Luni other than a 6,000-seat amphitheatre and a few sections of the old walls. Prominence in the marble industry passed to its neighbours, Massa and Carrara, two towns that have had a common history for a thousand years.

East of the Apuan Alps lies Garfagnana, a proud, wild and isolated valley which even the Romans never managed to dominate fully. Titus Livius said its inhabitants were "terrible people. The women here are as strong as men, while the men are as ferocious as wild beasts." Trapped between the foothills of the Apuan Alps and the first heights of the Tuscan-

The bridges of Vara, on the left bank of the Carrione. This is the heart of the marble region. A railway through here once linked the quarries of Fantiscritti, Ravaccione and Colonnati with the port of San Martino a Carrara. Many quarries are still in operation, providing, for example, the white marble of Battaglino, Canal Grande and Fantiscritti, as well as the Statuario di Betogli.

121

Emilian Apennines, Garfagnana has always been isolated from the activity of the nearby coast and from the main routes linking north and south. Thanks to this isolation the valley has preserved its forests, which still cover two-thirds of the region.

The landscape of Garfagnana features majestic mountains as well as gentle hills. Golden eagles nest in the Botri Canyon, at the bottom of which flow the crystal-clear waters of the Pelago River. Stags, roe deer, mountain goats and marmots inhabit the Orecchiella Nature Reserve, as do Italy's last surviving wolves.

Further south-east, where the Tuscan-Emilian and the Umbrian Apennines meet, the mountains are imbued with the mysticism of Saint Francis of Assisi and his disciples. Tuscan history, its golden Renaissance days as much as its mysterious Etruscan beginnings, is usually considered pagan. Tuscan artists, when dealing with religious subjects, tend to stress grace and elegance over devotion. Renaissance madonnas may receive angels and carry the infant Jesus in their arms – but they are draped in veils worthy of Aphrodite. This tendency has not changed with time; on the contrary, it seems ever stronger. Yet it must not be forgotten that this is also a land of faith, as is proudly exhibited by city cathedrals and village churches, tiny chapels scattered throughout the countryside, hermits' grottoes and countless other testimonies to religion and mysticism.

Castelnuovo di Garfagnana, at the confluence of the Turrite Secca and Serchio rivers, had great importance in the fifteenth century, when it put itself under the protection of the Estes, Lords of Ferrara, to avoid falling into the hands of Florence. The Florentines managed to seize it in 1512 with the help of Pope Leo X, but soon after the pope's death the people called back the Duke of Este, Alfonso I. Later captured by Napoleon, who merged it with the Cisalpine Republic, the town renewed its allegiance to its former lords, again recalling the Estes to power.

For eight centuries Monte La Verna, between the Arno and Tiber valleys, has been one focal point of this religious fervour. The mountain belonged to Count Orlando Cattini of Siena, lord of the Chiusi Castle and a notorious pleasure-seeker. In 1213 the count set off for San Leo in Romagna for a festival at which the son of his friend Buonconte da Montefeltro was to be knighted. There he met Saint Francis of Assisi and, after hearing him preach, immediately reformed and offered Francis and his disciples Monte La Verna. They put up a few cabins and built the small church of Santa Maria degli Angeli, where Francis would receive the stigmata. Two centuries later, a sanctuary was built next to the church and became one of the most famous in all Christendom. Today, despite the declining number of vocations, the monastery at La Verna – with its rich library, museum and crafts workshops – continues to flourish. Hundreds of Franciscan novices study and pray there and every year, thousands of pilgrims make their way to La Verna for the Feast of the Stigmata on 17 September and the Feast of Saint Francis on 4 October.

Like La Verna, the Camaldoli monastery is tucked into one of the beautiful beech and pine forests of Casentino. It was founded by Saint Romuald shortly after the year 1000 and built atop the ruins of the castle of Count Maldolo of Arezzo. It served as a hostel and hospice before being transformed into a monastery for hundreds of monks. Higher up in the forest is the hermitage to

A wild forest region of great beauty, though poor in natural resources, Garfagnana extends between the Apuans and the Apennines. Terraces are farmed below, sheep graze on the upper pastures and in between, towns such as this spread along the crests like ribbons of stone. For centuries, the principal form of nourishment here has been chestnuts.

A *former Benedictine monastery in the Apennines. The main building is still surrounded by the orderly rows of a vegetable garden. The rule of the Order, founded in the sixth century, prescribed both prayer and work ("ora et labora"). The presence of the Benedictines had a marked effect on the evolution of the Tuscan landscape.*

which Saint Romuald retreated and where the faithful still venerate a rock bearing handprints supposed to be those of the saint. It is said that Romuald clung desperately to this rock when Satan, furious at seeing him resist temptation, tried to fling him into the abyss below. In the fifteenth century, the monastery served as a meeting place for great humanists such as Lorenzo the Magnificent, the architect Leon Battista Alberti and the poet Cristoforo Landino.

South-east of Casentino, it becomes more difficult to distinguish the mountains from the hills. Between the Cecina and Ombrone valleys, for instance, one finds the *Colline Metallifere*, or Metal-Bearing Hills, so named although their approximately 1,000-metre altitude is closer to that of the Tuscan mountains. The name derives from the lodes of iron, zinc, lead, antimony and copper that provide the striking chromatic diversity of the soil. The Italian government recently decided to mine there in search of gold. But the hills are best known for the boraciferric *soffioni* of Montecerboli. It was the Frenchman Francis de Larderel who first thought of exploiting this steam, which shot up from the ground with the violence of a geyser, hiding everything in an

The Hermitage of Camaldoli, in the enchanted silence of the Casentino forest. It was here that Saint Romuald and his first four disciples built a small oratory and five tiny cells in 1012. In 1027 the oratory was replaced by the Church of the Holy Saviour (San Salvatore), later renovated in 1658. Adjoining the church is a library containing more than 10,000 volumes.

unreal fog pierced by strange noises like laments. The ancients believed that the steam escaped from the depths of Hades, into which the gods would drag anyone who might dare defy the geysers' threatening breath. In fact many miners, disoriented by the steam, have lost their way and never been seen again. Today the *soffioni* are exploited for their boric acid and geothermal energy, and the medieval ballad that tells the tale of Sapo Alberighi is no longer sung: this young knight disappeared into the mists while trying like Orpheus to save his Eurydice, who had been carried off to the Underworld. The modern age has left its mark, but the area's enchantment has not completely disappeared.

As one continues further south, the Tuscan mountains present their final spectacle: Monte Amiata. Here the line blurs not between mountain and hill but between mountain and volcano. The perfectly shaped cone of Amiata is a potent reminder of its volcanic origins; the volcano has been extinct since prehistoric times. The Romans called it *Mons ad Meata*, which means Mountain of Caverns, due to the highly porous nature of its rock, from which many springs still flow. Thanks to this abundance of water, grain, vineyards and olive trees have been planted around the foot of the volcano. Higher up, the slopes are covered with groves of chestnut and holm oak, while the snow-capped summit stands out against the sky. No other mountain in Tuscany is as striking as Monte Amiata, especially in April and May when it is cloaked in yellow broom, violets and light pink crocuses. It is equally resplendent when autumn's reds set ablaze its wooded slopes.

In the diary devoted to his travels in Italy, Henry James wrote that from afar, the Tuscan quarries looked like fortified cities on the mountain tops – cities that curiously failed to materialize as he drew closer. Seen from above, the mystery is explained: the "cities" James saw were really just blocks of roughly cut marble, waiting to be taken away.

A*quarry*
of Statuario marble. The Apuan
Alps have long been famous for
their marble, so brilliantly white
that the quarries, seen from
the sea, look like glaciers.
The Statuario di Carrara was
the preferred marble of
Michelangelo, and still today,
many sculptors choose it over
the marble from the Greek
archipelago – even over the
famed stone from Paros.

For thousands of years Apuan quarriers have worn out their bodies and risked their lives climbing these torturous curves. In older times, pegs of soft wood were introduced into slits in the marble and wetted so they would swell and cause the stone to split. The ancient Egyptians also used this prehistoric dynamite.

An impressive panorama over the ridges of the Apuan Alps, similar in name and form to the Alps but actually a separate chain. The Apuans are called alps simply because of their imposing aspect, though their altitudes are inferior to those of the Alps. The chain's highest peak is Monte ·Pisanino, which reaches a height of 1,945 metres above sea-level.

The dramatic Apuan Alps, their forbidding
peaks lost in the clouds, are home to the highest quarries. The Apuan marble industry
is more than 2,000 years old, and its primacy on the world market continues today:
annual production is more than 500,000 tons. Deposits are found throughout
the region, but those in the Carrione Valley, near Carrara, are particularly rich and
prized and account for 70 per cent of all Apuan production.

A panoramic view of Garfagnana, the valley extending to the west towards the Apuan Alps and to the north-east towards the Tuscan-Emilian Apennines and covering some 500 square kilometres. Some may be surprised to discover such an abundance of unspoiled greenery today, especially given the price Tuscany has paid environmentally to move from a predominantly agricultural economy to a mixed one. But the ecological preservation of Garfagnana is due less to governmental action than to the initiative of foreigners – Germans, British and Americans – who have saved thousands of acres by returning them to farmland.

The former fortress of Castelnuovo di
Garfagnana is today a picturesque grouping of towers, turrets, massive walls and
slender columns. In 1522 Alfonso I sent Ludovico Ariosto to rule this Este domain at
the lower boundary of Upper Garfagnana, a region of beautiful unspoiled spots like
the Parco dell'Orecchiella and spectacular panoramas such as the one
from San Pellegrino.

The Hermitage of Calomini, between
Aulla and Lucca, where, before the year 1000, a few monks lived in caves dug into the
rock. A small church was built to house an image of the Virgin which reportedly had
miraculous healing powers: thousands of faithful ascended the steep mountain –
the hermitage was located 360 metres above the plain – providing the monks with
the means to construct their monastery. The hermitage is still
an important pilgrimage site.

I n northern Tuscany one often encounters
tiny hamlets like this one, a few small houses surrounding a church in which Mass will
never again be celebrated. The exodus which began at the end of the Second World War
and continues today has severely reduced the populations of hundreds of villages.
Churches stay empty after old priests die, the faraway diocese being unable to replace
them. And so it is with schools: when a village has less than five children,
the doors are closed, never to reopen.

This village, clinging to a peak, is a perfect example of man's ingenuity in the face of limitations. The main street follows the crest, with houses lined up on either side, exploiting every available centimetre. Villages like this one have seen the departure of many of their young, an exodus that spells freedom for those who leave, but often the death of the hamlet they leave behind.

The magnificent mountain
vista of the Abetone, which boasts one of the Tuscan
Apennines' most famous ski resorts. Above: skiers setting
off. Numerous resorts have been built to cope with the
increasing crowds of winter visitors: it is now possible to
reach the great slopes of Monte Gomito (altitude: 1,892
metres) in a few minutes, as well as those, barely lower,
at Serrabassa and Regine.

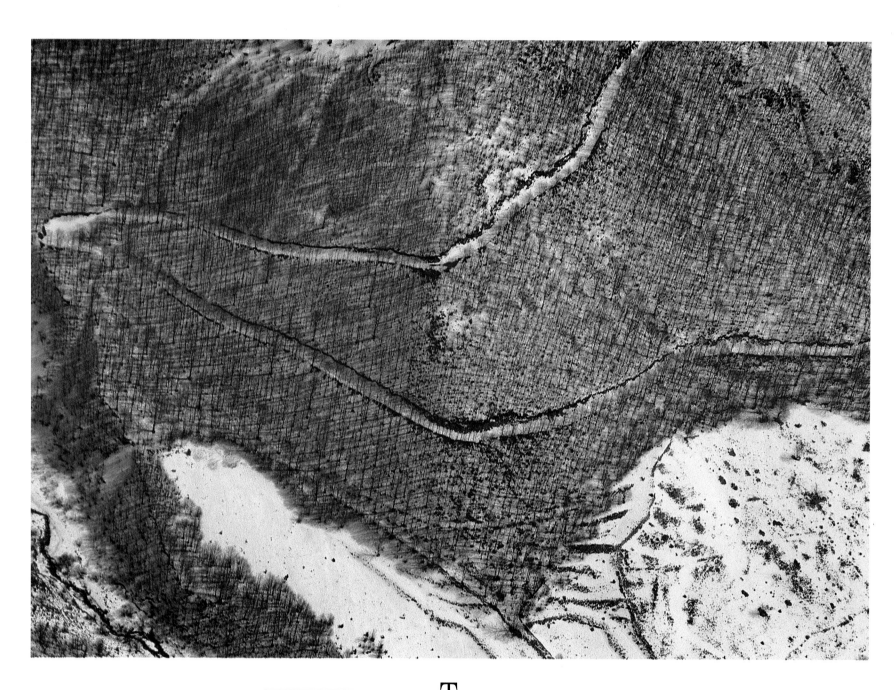

The Abetone forest. The woods in
this area, which includes the Emilian slopes to the north and the Tuscan side of the
Apennines to the south, have been famous since Etruscan times. The name, however,
is recent, dating from the second half of the nineteenth century, when the Grand Dukes
of Lorraine had a road built to join Emilia and Tuscany. This undertaking involved
chopping down an enormous pine tree (abetone in Italian), and
the name spread to the forest.

The lovely Abetone road, which climbs
from the Modena plain to a pass at 1,388 metres before descending again to La Lima
and the hills around Pistoia. There is a great variety of tourist spots within the area
now known as Abetone: from Fiumalba and Dogana Nuova on the Emilian slopes
to Serrabassa, Regine, Chiarofonte and Boscolungo on the Tuscan side. The road
is marked by two stone pyramids, noting that it owes its existence to the sovereigns
of Modena and Tuscany.

Farms in the Casentino region, north of Arezzo. Nearby are the sources of two great rivers, linked by history to two great cities: the Arno, which flows towards Florence, and the Tiber, which begins its journey to Rome. Of the two valleys, which are divided by a range of steep hills, the Arno's is more welcoming: the landscape is more varied, its many colours changing with the seasons.

143

Bands of lavender burst forth between
the dark green of the woods and the golden ochre of the soil. The Tuscan landscape
always has a few lovely surprises in store, especially in the upper valley of the Arno,
where lavender has been cultivated since Roman times. In those days it was used in the
distillation of the balsam oil with which one massaged guests after the ritual bath,
as well as by athletes. The flowered crests of these bushes are still gathered and put
into sachets for perfuming linen cupboards.

From the rolling countryside of the facing
page, we move into a landscape more rugged. This is the foot of the Pratomagno,
a long and unusual mountain chain which extends south-east of Florence, between the
Arno Valley and the Casentino. At one time the area was covered by a vast lake, which
has since dried up. Erosion has created a fantastic, almost lunar landscape here.

The calanchi of the Pratomagno region. A few years ago the discovery of a strange cave, approximately seven metres above ground-level, attracted many scientists to the region. They hoped to find subterranean dwellings, but they uncovered only the bones of a deer-like species which, according to radioactive carbon dating, were some 3,000 years old. Numerous traces of human settlements have been found nearby in the Arno Valley.

At first glance, this might seem to be just another Tuscan farm. However, the aerial photo reveals the ingenious renovation that transformed a fortified castle into a home for peacetime. In the foreground, the fortified dwelling dominated the walls and banks. Just behind is the chapel, and behind that, the principal tower of the complex from which the minor feudal lord governed his few subjects. We are in the environs of Reggello, a territory dominated, between the thirteenth and fifteenth centuries, by the powerful Counts of Guidi di Poppi.

The monastery at Camaldoli, which was built as a hospice for the hermitage shown on page 125. The first building was erected atop the remains of the former Fontebuona castle of Count Maldolo d'Arezzo. Others were added, eventually forming the impressive complex revealed in this photograph. Burned and sacked on numerous occasions, the monastery always managed to rise from its ashes, attaining a real splendour between the sixteenth and seventeenth centuries. At that time, it even had its own printing press and was the site of a humanist academy whose members included Lorenzo the Magnificent and Leon Battista Alberti, a leading architect.

The mountain of La Verna where, on 17 September 1224, Saint Francis of Assisi received the stigmata. The mountain belonged to Orlando Cattani, a pleasure-loving nobleman who reformed after hearing Francis preach. The very same day, he gave the mountain and woods to Francis who, with his companions, constructed a few log cabins with roofs of foliage. The saint returned to the mountain six times, between 1214 and 1224. The monastery became the property of the municipality of Florence upon the suppression of religious orders, but was returned to the Order of the Frati Minori in 1933 with the Lateran Pact between the Italian State, represented by Mussolini, and the Holy See.

149

T*alamone, at the southern edge of the Monti dell'Uccellina, was an active Etruscan port and later a Roman naval base. Repeatedly destroyed by wars and pirate attacks (it was sacked in 1544 by the infamous Red Beard), the town was seriously damaged during the Allied invasion of Italy. Today it is a modern vacation centre. Little remains of the picturesque old fishing village, and only a medieval castle (seen in the lower left of the photograph) evokes the many centuries of Talamone's forgotten history.*

THE
COASTS

Two thousand years ago, geologists say, the coast of Tuscany lay some six kilometres further inland from where it is today. Over time, marine erosion has been more than counteracted by the build-up of deposits in the fluvial plains. The coast stretches for 300 kilometres between Liguria and Latium, and contains no mountains or hills. The Tuscan littoral has nine rivers: from north to south the Magra, Serchio, Arno, Cecina, Cornia, Bruna, Ombrone, Albegna and Flora. All are torrential, and their flows can become violent without warning. The accumulation of deposits has modelled the scenery into vast bays rimmed with dunes, leaving only the occasional rocky outcrop, like an outpost of the mountains found inland.

The colour of the Tyrrhenian Sea off Tuscany is not the uniform dark blue of the Ligurian Sea. The Tyrrhenian's depths are deeper, its currents stronger. Its spectrum ranges from the palest of hues to an almost-black Prussian blue. During the violent storms unleashed by the *libeccio*, the merciless wind that blows from the south-west, the immense sea appears a mustard colour near the shore, then a Nile green further out, and finally a deep blue extending to the horizon to meet the leaden clouds. The thousand blues of this sea are echoed in the myriad greens of the Mediterranean underbrush. Arbutus, heather, pistachio, myrtle and broom surround trunks of oak, holm oak and cork, or spill over a carpet of rosemary, lavender, asparagus and other fragrant plants. Even the unbridled depredations of real-estate speculation have not succeeded in wiping out this fantastic botanical universe, with its pervasive perfume.

Just as the emblem of the hills is the cypress, along the coast it is the pine. What were once sea and Syrian pines have today largely been replaced by a domesticated subspecies. Whereas the underbrush is primarily spontaneous vegetation, the pine forests are almost totally the work of man, planted behind the beaches to shield

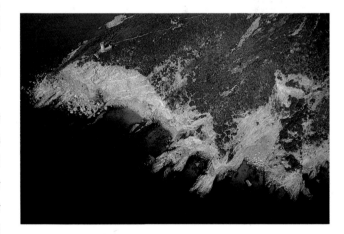

cultivations in the hinterlands from salty winds. The pine forests offer a peaceful transition between land and water, even more restful and refreshing to those coming from Liguria, where the rocky cliffs drop sharply to the sea.

The flat and easily accessible Tuscan coast is ideally suited to the development of resorts, and many there have earned an international reputation. To the north, the Versilian Riviera is one vast, dazzling tourist attraction. Old fishing villages such as Forte dei Marmi, Pietrasanta, Le Focette and Camaiore have melted into a string of villas, hotels, pensions, restaurants, pizzerias, tennis courts and riding centres that stretches from Massa to Viareggio. The latter

White rocks descend into the water along the Argentario coast, a large promontory which over thousands of years has become separated from the mainland. Only two narrow sandy strips, called còrdoli and barely 400 metres wide, still attach it to the coast. Between them extends the Orbetello Lagoon, on the edge of Latium. It was from here that Italo Balbo's Italian seaplanes took off to cross the Atlantic in formation, a first in aviation history.

The Monti dell'Uccellina, one of the few fully protected nature preserves in Italy. The vegetation is abundant and varied. The Mediterranean underbrush is crossed only by vague paths: if not for the reliable reference of the sea one could easily get lost today, as happened to people for centuries. Around the year 1000 Benedictine hermits arrived in this setting of silence and contemplation and built the Abbey of San Rabano.

was internationally famous even before its association with the Eurovision song contest, thanks to its picturesque carnival, in which a parade of allegorical floats provides an excellent opportunity for citizens to voice their atavistic Tuscan irreverence.

Versilia ends at the mouth of the Serchio, the beginning of the Pisan Riviera, which continues to Leghorn and includes Marina di Pisa and Tirrenia. If every Tuscan city is a planet with only a few traits in common with the rest of the constellation, then it must be said that Leghorn is particularly incompatible – and particularly proud of its individuality. The Livornese even have their own dialect, pronouncing "R" as "L". This sense of self doubtless results from the city's history, beginning with the progressive silting-up of the maritime port at Pisa, which made Leghorn the principal port in Tuscany. Passed from the Pisans to the Genoese to the Florentines, Leghorn regained its importance under the Medici, who made it second only to Florence. The imposing structures of the Medici port – an important trading and industrial centre since its completion in 1618 – are still worthy of

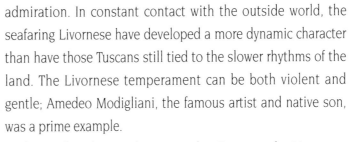

admiration. In constant contact with the outside world, the seafaring Livornese have developed a more dynamic character than have those Tuscans still tied to the slower rhythms of the land. The Livornese temperament can be both violent and gentle; Amedeo Modigliani, the famous artist and native son, was a prime example.

Above all and more than any other Tuscans, the Livornese are incapable of resisting a good practical joke. Where else but in Leghorn would youths – as three did several years ago – arm themselves with a Black & Decker and sculpt stone heads in the style of Modigliani, then dump them into a canal? When these "artworks" were "discovered", the most illustrious experts solemnly identified them as originals before the perpetrators revealed the hoax to the media.

South of Leghorn there are a number of famous beaches – Quercianella, Castiglioncello, Rosignano and Vada – before one reaches the mouth of the Cecina and thus arrives in the Maremma. This is a region difficult to categorize; as Gertrude Stein supposedly said, "The Maremma is the Maremma." At one time, "Maremma" was a synonym for any mosquito-infested marshland whose inhabitants suffered from malaria. Or from insanity brought on by solitude, as happened to the protagonist of a famous novel by Renato Fucini. One might go to the marshes for a day or at most two to hunt wild duck. Today nearly all the Maremman marshes have disappeared – and with them the malaria – following three centuries of drainage efforts. But the landscape which

The Uccellina
Nature Park extends to the
southern limit of the Tuscan
Riviera, some fifteen kilometres
in length and five in width.
In this stretch the landscape
becomes softer, its woods
descending gently to the sea;
elsewhere, rocky cliffs drop
straight to the water and the
magnificent landscapes can
only be appreciated from a boat.
To the north, at Paduletto,
is the only true beach, which
is overlooked by the Torre
del Collelungo.

Motor launches and sailboats at anchor in the small port of Viareggio, with its vast beach just behind. This is the largest seaside resort on the Tyrrhenian Sea and one of the largest in Italy. Its success as a vacation spot goes back to 1861, when Giuseppe Barellai founded his Ospizi Marini (marine hospices) here, the first structures to accommodate vacationers. The undertaking encountered not a few early obstacles, as it was considered immoral for men and women to see each other in bathing costume!

appears and disappears between reeds and marsh grass, swathed in veils of mist, has lost none of its old magic. The Maremma is famous for its legendary *butteri*, riders who once boasted of never dismounting, not even on their wedding night (when the bride was expected to climb into the saddle). Whereas the American cowboy is a figure of the frontier, of the quest for new horizons, the Maremman *buttero* rides day and night but never

leaves the Maremma, where he raises livestock and hunts hare or partridge. Buffalo Bill Cody's cowboys did challenge the *butteri* at the start of the century. But by then Buffalo Bill was just a circus impresario, and this riding contest was no epic encounter. (For the record, the Italians won.)

In the Maremma, which marks the southern end of the Tuscan coast, there are fewer beach resorts than one finds further north. Most of the tourists who arrive at Piombino embark for Elba and the other islands of the Tuscan archipelago. But the Maremman coast, from Follonica to Punta Ala, from Castiglione della Pescaia to Marina di Grosseto and as far as the Argentario Peninsula, is far from deserted. Its tourism tends to be concentrated into large, integrated resort pockets, unlike the beach-umbrella-blanketed Versilian coast.

The city of Grosseto lies twelve kilometres in from the coast, but its history is linked more closely with the sea than with the land. The town was founded by the inhabitants of Roselle, who fled from that flourishing Etruscan maritime port when it was destroyed by the Saracens in 935. Grosseto developed rapidly, eventually becoming capital of the Maremma, and in 1138 Pope Innocent II established a rich and prestigious bishopric there. Constantly battling a withdrawing sea, which left behind lagoons and swamps, Grosseto finally managed to eke out a vital space through reclamation. This drainage work was begun by Benedictine monks around the year 1000, and continued by the Medici, the Grand Dukes of Lorraine and the Savoy monarchy. It was ultimately completed after the founding of the Republic.

South of Grosseto is the Uccellina Nature Park, with its superb views across the sea to the Tuscan archipelago. Close by is the site of the castle of Collecchio, whose inhabitants were massacred by the ferocious Khair-ad-Din, better known as Red Beard, during the night of 22 April 1543. The sole survivor, Margherita Marsili, was sixteen, blonde, beautiful – and resolved. She was led off to the Sultan's harem to become one of approximately 200 concubines. But she survived and was eventually promoted to principal wife – after, it is said, having poisoned two rivals.

The beach at Forte dei Marmi, one of the trendiest beach resorts of the Tyrrhenian coast. The region, at the foot of the Apuan Alps, offers a serene holiday look: hotels, boarding houses, mansions and vacation homes follow one another in an unbroken line along the sea. Here development has not run rampant – the buildings are still low enough that the pine forests usually manage to at least partially hide the settlements. The fortress of the name, which still stands on the principal piazza, was constructed in 1788 by Grand Duke Leopoldo of Lorraine and provided the original nucleus of the town.

155

A panoramic view of the centre of Leghorn. The Fosso Reale or Royal Channel, a navigable canal, still links the Darsena (Old Basin), the New Fortress, the Old Fortress and the Medici port. The city centre, a pentagon-shaped area containing the Duomo and administration buildings, is thus isolated, like a castle surrounded by its moat.

The Fosso Reale, which once surrounded the city walls, offers unusual perspectives on the urban design of Leghorn. The city was almost completely destroyed by Allied bombing during the Second World War, and has been rebuilt according to the original plans to preserve, as much as possible, the look of the past. Monuments also have been reconstructed, with the same eye to authenticity.

The Duomo and
the Piazza Dante, in the centre
of Grosseto. The cathedral was
constructed between 1294 and
1302 by Sozzo di Rustichino
atop the remains of an earlier
church. The brick bell-tower
dates from 1402 but was
extensively modified in 1600
and again in 1911. At
the centre of the piazza is a
monument to Leopoldo II
(1846), erected in recognition
of his fight against malaria in
Tuscany. The piazza was
nicknamed "Il Cisternone"
by the people, due to the large
water tank (cisterna) which
the Dukes of Lorraine had dug
to collect water from
an Artesian well.

The industrial harbour of Leghorn, protected by four large breakwaters: the Curvilinea to the right in the photograph, the Meloria, the Marzocco and the Vigliaia. The port extends to the Old Harbour, the former Medici port, and to the Mandraccio Basins, which are primarily commercial. Shipping activity in Leghorn has reached 7,000 arrivals and departures per year, accounting for the movement of more than ten million tons of merchandise.

The intimate cove of Quercianella,
a beach resort on the Tuscan coast south of Leghorn. The breakwater of large boulders
partially closes the entrance, thus permitting pleasure boats to remain at anchor when
seas are rough. It also represents a safeguard of the bay's current aspect, one of the
most beautiful in this stretch of coast: the ocean currents would wipe out an
unprotected beach in a few decades.

The coast south of Leghorn is very different
from that to the north: the sand disappears and waves break against wild rocks,
the final manifestations of the inland mountain chains. Numerous watchtowers were
built along this stretch of coast, such as the Torre di Calafuria, the Torre del Boccale
and the Torre del Romito, between the fourteenth and seventeenth centuries
to guard against Barbary pirates.

The castle of Quercianella, tucked into pine
woods. These dense forests afford a pleasant coolness even on the hottest summer days.
Nearby Castiglioncello offers beaches harmoniously divided into coves such as
Marina di Campolecciano, Portovecchio and Caletta.

T*he pine forest of San Rossore, six kilometres from Pisa. Previously an imperial forest, it passed into the hands of the Bishop of Pisa, then to the Medici, who constructed a large farm here. Upon the unification of Italy the forest became a royal hunting preserve for the recreation of the House of Savoy; it later became the property of the president of the Republic. The holding extends over 3,000 hectares; among the many animals who live there in liberty – deer, stag, boar – are a few dromedaries which were brought from the African colonies in homage to Victor Emmanuel III.*

This may look like the Amazonian rain forest, but it is the Uccellina Nature Park. The Mediterranean underbrush, dense and perfumed, quietly besieges ancient watchtowers while ivy covers the picturesque ruins of the Abbey of San Rabano. This paradise, devoid of any modern settlement, is an oasis where wild animals such as deer, boar, badger, otter, fox and even wildcat can breed in peace.

*O*ne of
the marble-loading jetties
at Marina di Carrara.
The harbour is located at the
centre of a large beach, between
the mouths of the Carrione and
Parmignola rivers. Popular
bathing resorts extend on both
sides of the commercial port.
Traffic is heavy, especially
considering that there is only
one kind of merchandise being
traded: in 1989 a total of
1.5 million tons of marble was
extracted, of which 528,379
tons were exported by sea.

A typical fishermen's trabucco at the mouth
of the Arno. The traditional fishing method employs a net, called a bilancia after
its resemblance to a scale, which is put into the water on a long beam like an enormous
fishing pole. When the net is spread across the sea-bed the fish swim above it without
the least suspicion – until the beam suddenly raises the net at all four corners.

T*he harbour of Talamone. The ancient castle and the outline of the walls that once surrounded the fortress and the entire village are still visible. The location was so favourable that the Sienese, having become lords of Talamone in 1303, planned to make it into a commercial maritime and military port of call to rival Pisa and Genoa. Many scorned this overly ambitious project, including Dante in The Divine Comedy.*

The Spanish fort at Porto Ercole on the Orbetello Lagoon. The star-shaped plan of the fortifications is typical of the sixteenth century, when firearms had just been introduced but had not yet produced a revision in military architecture. Later, walls were rounded to resist the ever-more powerful artillery projectiles.

A stretch of the southern coast of the island of Elba, at the foot of Monte Calamita or Mount Magnet, so called because its large quantities of ferrous ore disrupt compass needles. The whole island is rich in mineral deposits. It has been established that iron was mined here prior to the Greek conquest, and its exploitation continues. In 1870, annual production totalled barely 100,000 tons; today it is five times greater. The ore is smelted in the blast furnaces of Piombino, Genoa, Naples and Trieste.

THE
ISLANDS

Among its many riches, Tuscany even boasts its own archipelago. There are seven islands – Elba, Montecristo, Pianosa, Capraia, Gorgona, Giglio and Giannutri – ranking in beauty and charm with the mainland. Millions of years ago, these islands were simply peaks of the western Apennines. Having reduced them to promontories, the sea then cut them off from what is now the coast, conferring upon them a destiny of splendour and silence – to which man added a punitive element. Five of the seven islands have held prisoners, the most famous being Napoleon at Elba.

By 1000 BC, the Ligurians and Greeks were exploiting the iron deposits in Rio Terranera and La Calamita on Elba. The principal island was given its first name, Aethena, by the Greeks. They were followed by the Etruscans, who were also attracted by the mineral deposits. Finally came the Romans, who appreciated the island's charm and mild climate, the rocky coast plunging to the sea and the harmonious plains where olive groves alternated with vineyards. (Wine from Elba was particularly prized in Rome; in order to drink it properly chilled the Romans dug cellars ten metres deep and filled them with snow). The Romans renamed the island Ilva and built fabulous villas there, ruins of which can still be seen. One villa, at Grotte di Portoferraio, boasted an elegant pool – the fifth-largest of all those built by the Romans. It was fed by an ingenious hydraulic system which provided rose-scented hot water so that the nobleman and his guests could bathe even in winter. There are also remains of villas at Capo Castello, Falcria and Pomonte, while others, along the east coast, still await excavation.

After the Roman era, Elba was invaded frequently: by Lombards, Pisans, Genoese, Spanish, French, English and, at regular intervals, Saracen pirates. The archipelago was no longer considered a place for pleasure. Even romantic travellers on the Grand Tour, who explored almost every Tuscan road in search of beauty and the past, tended to overlook the islands. Elba came under the European spotlight between May 1814 and February 1815, during Napoleon's exile there. It then sank back into oblivion until the 1950s, when tourism began to develop, feeding on the island's Napoleonic history. Since then tourist coaches have stopped religiously in front of every cliff, bridge, house, fountain and tree where, according to the guides, the emperor supposedly once strolled and meditated. The old mill on the heights above Portoferraio, where Napoleon held court for the last time, is now a museum and one of the island's principal tourist attractions.

It was at Elba that deep-sea diving was first practised as a sport. Italian sailors returning home after the Second World War brought along their flippers, goggles and diving suits. Until then, such equipment had been employed only for military ends; no one had imagined it

Pianosa owes its name (piano means flat) to its geography: the highest point is 27 metres above sea-level. Fourteen kilometres from Elba, the island covers ten square kilometres. The discovery of fossil remains of bears and deer confirmed the hypothesis that about 500,000 years ago, the island was joined to the mainland. To visit the penal colony here requires permission from the government.

173

might be used for fun. But diving and underwater fishing proved to be easy and exhilarating, and the island's clear waters were teeming with fish. The huge success of this sport spawned hotels, restaurants and all the accompaniments.

The island of Montecristo, on the other hand, remains undeveloped, thanks to its status as a nature preserve. The scenery today is much as it was in 1829 when Alexandre Dumas imagined Edmond Dantès, *The Count of Montecristo*, searching there for the treasure cave. The island is composed of a single block of granite, its three peaks thrusting into the sky above the dark-green Mediterranean underbrush. On the highest peak are the remains of a fortress built by the Lords of Piombino; to the north-east are the ruins of the monastery of San Salvatore e San Massimiliano. According to legend, the monks hid the fabulous treasures of a wealthy cardinal there. This tale was a source of inspiration for Dumas as well as for the Turkish pirate Dragut, who – in vain – attacked the island no less than seven times in pursuit of the treasure. Finally, in 1553, the monks fled to the mainland. Paradoxically, this present-

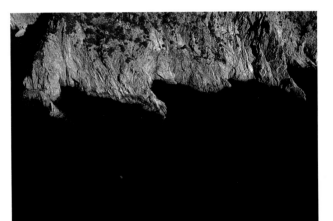

day sanctuary for Mediterranean fauna was once the hunting reserve of Victor Emmanuel II of Savoy. The island also has served as a penal colony; along the sixteen kilometres of rocky coast there is only one, easily guarded approach, at Cala Maestra.

In contrast to the wild peaks of Montecristo, Pianosa is a plain barely rising above sea-level. The island owes its name to its geography, which is unique in the archipelago; the Romans called it *Planasia*. Its fields of grain and vineyards punctuated by olive trees, cactus and asphodels form a landscape as gentle as its history is violent. It was here that the Roman Emperor Augustus exiled his nephew Postumius, who was suspected of treason.

Today one can visit the ruins of the luxurious villa in which Postumius stayed only briefly; he was assassinated shortly after his arrival. Twice – at the hands of the Genoese and of the Turks under Kara Mustafa – the population was sold into bondage and deported. Pianosa remained deserted until the nineteenth century, when the government established a prison there too.

Capraia, on the other hand, has hills covered with dense vegetation, the volcanic origins of which are easily recognizable. Its name apparently derives from the wild goats (*capra*) which once inhabited the island. Palaeontologists have found abundant fossilized remains of bears and the forerunners of deer and horses, dating from before the archipelago was cut off from the mainland. But here, as on Pianosa, the development of tourism has been hindered by the presence of yet another prison. Gorgona has a similar tale to tell.

The landscape of Gorgona is marvellously varied: to the north are high, inaccessible rocks

Another aspect of the coast of Giglio, which boasts greenery running down to the edge of the sea. The island has long been famous for the production of a strong, aromatic wine, Ansonaco, and for an abundance of game. Even today one finds wild rabbit, grey partridge and woodcock here. It was off this coast, in the thirteenth century, that the fleet of Emperor Frederick II destroyed the Genoese ships that were carrying the prelates summoned to Rome by Pope Gregory IX for a council against the Empire.

175

F orte Focardo at Porto Azzurro, on the eastern coast of Elba. It is said that the name Focardo stems from the fire (fuoco) lit atop one of the towers that served as a lighthouse for navigators. The massive structure was erected by the Spanish in 1678 to secure their domination of the island, which was menaced by French expansion.

and to the east, rolling hills covered with pines, olives, cypresses, oaks and chestnuts. These species were introduced before 1000 AD by Benedictine monks who sought refuge there. Remains of their monasteries can still be seen. The island had flourished at the time of the Phoenicians (who called it Urgon), and was an important trading port under the Etruscans and the Romans. In the eighth century AD, the Lombard King Desiderius came here in great pomp to recover the remains of Saint Julia (who had been martyred three centuries earlier in Corsica) and take them back to Brescia. The saint's body was supposed to have remained miraculously intact.

The two southernmost islands have been spared a penal role. Arriving at Giglio from Porto Santo Stefano, one is greeted by a symphony of shapes and colours. From afar, the island has the profile of a mountain and its coast seems rugged. But closer up, one discovers sheltered coves with sandy beaches – at Arenella, Cannelle, Giglio Porto and, on the other side of the island, the even larger and more appealing beach of Campese. Giglio's attractions are numerous: the climate is extraordinarily mild (temperatures never fall below freezing or rise above 25°c); the flora is lush with pine, chestnut, oak, olive and fig trees, and the wildlife – hare, rabbit, tern, woodcock – is abundant. Even the sole reptile found on the island – the *coluber viridiflavus* – is a totally harmless snake, as if in homage to so gentle a spot. During the Roman era, the powerful Enobarbi family, ancestors of Nero, used to spend holidays in a villa on Giglio; its remains are still visible. Next arrived monks from northern Europe, followed by nobles and governors from Rome, Perugia, Pisa and Florence, then, finally, Alphonse of Aragon. In 1544, the island was sacked by the legendary Red Beard, who enslaved all 700 inhabitants. Today, Giglio's history lives on in the high medieval ramparts, watchtowers, narrow streets and mysterious lairs of the town of Giglio Castello.

A few miles away, the island of Giannutri mirrors, though on a lesser scale, the geography and history of Giglio. The relief is less dramatic, and the coast has only two small pebble beaches, Cala Maestra and Cala dello Spalmatoio. The ruins of a jetty at the former and of a port at the latter attest to the period when the Romans maintained a naval base there. Following the coast north of Cala Maestra one encounters the remains of cisterns, storehouses, baths, a governor's residence and servants' quarters. There is also the ruin of a splendid villa built by the Enobarbi, with superb mosaics and glistening white marble columns. Closing our eyes here, we can easily picture the Romans gathered for a banquet, the tones of zithers and lutes floating gently above their conversation as they sip the wines of Ansonaco, Falerno and Syria.

The harbour of Capraia. The harsh nature of the terrain and the presence of a penal colony make it more pleasurable to see Capraia from the sea than from the land. A sea-tour of the island enables one to admire wild and usually inaccessible landscapes, and to discover the many grottoes dug into the overhanging rock face. Until a few years ago, some of these housed a colony of monk seals.

P̲almaiola, one islet of the Tuscan
archipelago, near the coast of Elba. Its sole structure is a lighthouse. Maritime traffic,
today all touristic, was primarily commercial until the end of the Second World War.
The Genoese imported wine and sugar via sailboats which were still in service at
the end of the 1930s. Steamboats – and eventually diesel – were reserved
for the transport of iron ore.

The islet called
Lo Scoglietto, or Little Rock.
The islet faces the Forte della
Stella at Portoferraio on Elba.
The fort was constructed in
1548 by Cosimo I de' Medici,
who had seized the port and
some surrounding terrain from
Giacomo IV Appiano. As of
1751 Portoferraio was the
principal base of the Grand
Duchy of Tuscany's fleet.

The sheltered harbour of Portoferraio on Elba. In the upper left, the imposing mass of the Forte della Stella, so named for the five-pointed shape (stella means star) of its walls. One of its towers was transformed into a lighthouse. It was here that Napoleon was imprisoned from May 1814 to February 1815, when he returned to France for a final revenge – and definitive defeat.

The basin of Porto Azzurro, along the southeast coast of Elba. The name was given during the Fascist period to improve the image of a region known to Italians as Porto Longone, a sort of Mediterranean Alcatraz. The penitentiary is still functioning but has been transformed into a model prison in which inmates can work in a factory; with the profits, the prisoners have been able to restore and modernize their cells, which were the first in Italy to boast hygienic facilities.

181

A *panoramic view of the island of Capraia. In the upper left, a Genoese watchtower; to the right is the San Giorgio Fortress shown closer up on the facing page. Coach service is available from the small harbour to the top of the island. The Bellavista Piazza affords a splendid view of Elba and, on clear days, as far as Montecristo.*

A close-up view of the San Giorgio Fortress at Capraia, built by the Genoese ninety metres above sea-level. The rock precipice provided a natural defence against attackers – until the Saracens seized the island around the year 1000. They were later driven off by the infantry of the Republic of Pisa following a furious battle.

A characteristic view of the coast of Giglio, which lies only fourteen kilometres from the Argentario Massif, on the border of Tuscany and Latium. Despite strong winds and infrequent rain, the Mediterranean underbrush still grows vigorously on the rock, lending green to an evocative landscape. This point looks like the head and flipper of a tortoise emerging from its shell.

A low-flying view of the Torre del Campese, a former watchtower on Giglio. Among the island's attractions are small beaches of soft sand and crystal-clear depths of water. One can even walk barefoot on this type of rock.

185

The Sparviero, or Sparrowhawk, Rock,
located in the Gulf of Follonica facing Ala Point and Castiglione della Pescaia.
On this arid rock, battered by a relentless sun, stands a watchtower on which the
inhabitants of the mainland coast kept their eyes trained day and night,
in fear of a Saracen attack.

Unlike the
island of Pianosa, Montecristo
is characterized by cliffs that
plunge directly to the sea. The
island's highest peak, the Picco
della Fortezza, rises 645 metres
above sea-level. Legend holds
that in the fifth century, Saint
Maximilian, Bishop of Palermo,
fled the persecution of the
Vandals and took refuge here.
Now owned by the government,
Montecristo has become
a nature preserve.

187

Gorgona, the northernmost
island of the Tuscan archipelago. In the early days
of Christianity, monks from all around the Mediterranean
sought refuge here. In 1400 the island came under the
dominion of the Medici, who undertook construction of
a vast defence system, including the fortress seen in the
photograph above. In the foreground are terraces dug by
the Benedictines for the cultivation of their crops.

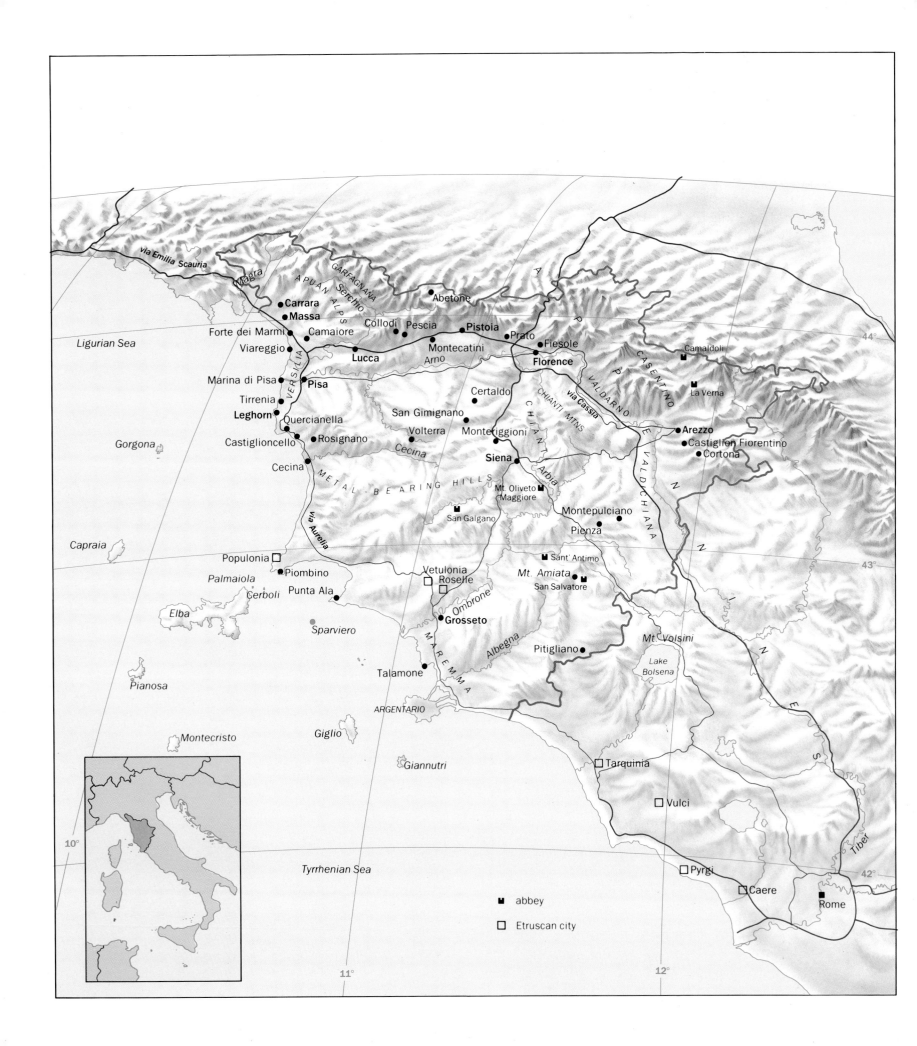

Ligurian Sea

via Emilia Scauria

Magra

GARFAGNANA

Serchio

APUAN ALPS

Carrara
Massa

Forte dei Marmi
Camaiore
Collodi
Pescia
Montecatini
Abetone
Pistoia
Prato
Fiesole

Viareggio
Lucca
Arno
Florence

Marina di Pisa
Pisa

Tirrenia
Leghorn
Quercianella

Castiglioncello
Rosignano

Cecina
Cecina

Certaldo
San Gimignano
Volterra
Monteriggioni

CHIANTI MTNS

via Cassia
VALDARNO

CASENTINO

Camaldoli

La Verna

Arezzo
Castiglion Fiorentino
Cortona

Siena
Arbia

METAL-BEARING HILLS

Mt. Oliveto Maggiore

San Galgano

Montepulciano
Pienza

VALDICHIANA

via Aurelia

Populonia
Piombino
Punta Ala

Vetulonia
Roselle

Sant' Antimo

Mt. Amiata
San Salvatore

Grosseto
Ombrone

MAREMMA

Albegna

Pitigliano

Mt. Volsini

Lake Bolsena

Talamone

ARGENTARIO

Gorgona

Capraia

Palmaiola
Cerboli

Elba

Sparviero

Pianosa

Montecristo

Giglio

Giannutri

Tyrrhenian Sea

Tarquinia

Vulci

Pyrgi

Caere

Rome

Tiber

■ abbey
□ Etruscan city

10°
11°
12°
44°
43°
42°

SELECT BIBLIOGRAPHY

LITERATURE

Boccaccio, Giovanni, *The Decameron*, trans. G.H. McWilliam, 1972
Conaway, *Julia Bondanella and Mark Musa* (eds), The Italian Renaissance Reader, 1987
King, Francis, *Florence : A Literary Companion*, 1991
Lawrence, D.H., *Etruscan Places*, in D.H. Lawrence and Italy, 1985
Machiavelli, Niccolò, *The Prince*, trans. G. Bull, 1961
Mortimer, John, *Summer's Lease*, 1988
Raison, Laura, (ed), *Tuscany : An Anthology*, 1983
Tozzi, Federigo, *Eyes Shut : A Novel*, trans. Kenneth Cox, 1990

GUIDES

Acton, Harold and Edward Chaney, *Florence : A traveller's Companion*, 1986
Bentley, James, *A Guide to Tuscany*, 1988
Keates, Jonathan and Charlie Waite, *Tuscany*, 1988
Macadam, Alta, *Blue Guide : Northern Italy*, 1991
Michelin Tourist Guide, *Italy*, 1991

HISTORY

Brion, Marcel, *The Medici : A Great Florentine Family*, trans G. and H. Cremonesi, 1980
Burckhardt, J., *The Civilization of the Renaissance in Italy*, trans. S.G.C. Middlemore, 1990
Einstein, L., *The Tuscan Garden*, 1927
Green, Julien, *God's Fool : The Life and Times of Francis of Assisi*, trans. Peter Hainegg, 1986
Hale, J.R., *Florence and the Medici*, 1986
Hay, Denys and John Law, *Italy in the Age of the Renaissance*, 1989
Lucas - Dubreton, Jean, *Daily Life in Florence in the Time of the Medici*, trans. A. Lytton Sells, 1960
Machiavelli, Niccolò, *History of Florence and of the Affairs of Italy*, 1960
McCarthy, Mary, *The Stones of Florence*, 1972
Norwich, John, Julius, *The Italian World*, 1983
Pallottino, Massimo, *The Etruscans*, trans. J. Cremona, 1975
Sismondi, Simonde de, *History of the Italian Republics*, 1906

ART

Acton, Harold, *The Villas of Tuscany*, 1984
Berenson, Bernard, *The Passionate Sightseer*, 1988
Chastel, André, *Art of the Italian Renaissance*, trans. L. and P. Murray, 1988
Hale, J.R. (ed), *Encyclopaedia of the Italian Renaissance*, 1981
Hartt, Frederick, *A History of Italian Renaissance Art*, 1988
Murray, Peter, *The Architecture of the Italian Renaissance*, 1986
Pallotino, Massimo, *Art of the Etruscans*, 1955
Vasari, Giorgio, *Lives of the Painters, Sculptors and Architects*, trans. A.B. Hinds, 1963

Chiusi, on the southern edge of the Valdichiana. Though its buildings only partially reveal the outline of its original urban plan, its extraordinary past as powerful Etruscan settlement is amply illustrated by documents in the National Museum, as well as in the necropolises that surround the city.

AKNOWLEDGMENTS

Guido Alberto Rossi wishes to thank the pilot, Commander Enzo Bianchini, with whom he took all the photographs, and Gianluigi Scarfiotti, an old friend and valuable guide who gave generously of his hospitality and his assistance in discovering many marvellous spots in Tuscany. The editors wish to thank Cesare Ciucchi, flight instructor, as well as everyone else who contributed precious assistance in the creation of this work.

All the photographs have received SMA publication authorization

no 0071 of 21 January 1990 and no 0773 of 3 july 1990